YOU SIMPLY HIT THEM WITH AN AXE

Other books written or edited by Tony Ring:

Plum Stones (Galahad Books, 1993)
* Wodehouse in the Clubhouse (1994)
* Wodehouse at the Anglers' Rest (1995)

* Books forming part of The Millennium Wodehouse Concordance, an eight-part series published by Porpoise Books, scheduled to be completed by 2001

Books relating to P G Wodehouse
published by Porpoise Books

A Man of Means
   by P G Wodehouse and C H Bovill (1991)
The Reminiscences of the Hon. Galahad
Threepwood
   edited by N T P Murphy (1993)

YOU SIMPLY HIT THEM

WITH AN AXE

*The extraordinary true story of the tax turmoils
of P G Wodehouse*

by

TONY RING

PORPOISE BOOKS

© A J Ring 1995
who asserts his rights as author of this book

Cover design and layout by Brian Sanderson

Printed by Antony Rowe Limited, Chippenham, England

A CIP catalogue record for this book
is available from the British Library

Porpoise Books
68 Altwood Road
Maidenhead
SL6 4PZ
UK

ISBN 1 870304 22 5

YOU SIMPLY HIT THEM WITH AN AXE

CONTENTS

FOOTNOTES are explained at the end of each chapter.

REFERENCES, unless otherwise indicated, are to UK first editions.

ACKNOWLEDGEMENTS

Assistance has been received from a wide range of people in the preparation of this book. I should mention first Arthur Andersen & Co, for it was while I was in that firm's employment in 1970 that I first learned of the US tax cases involving P G Wodehouse, and it seems somehow appropriate that their London Office head of US personal taxation, Walter Meisenkothen, has kindly read the manuscript and helped me avoid the most culpable technical errors.

Gathering material always required cooperation from libraries, and thanks go to Sally Brown at the Modern and Literary Manuscripts Department of the British Library for arranging access to a number of items including the LCP copies of various stage productions; to the Rare Book and Manuscript Library at Columbia University in New York, for access to the Paul Revere Reynolds collection of correspondence with Wodehouse; and to my local Great Missenden Library, especially Amanda Avery, who tracked down a number of out of print books through the invaluable inter-library loan system.

Grateful thanks are due to those who have given consent to use quotations from material within their ownership or copyright, including: Weidenfeld and Nicolson, publishers of *A Twentieth Century Life* and *Evelyn Waugh — Portrait of a Country Neighbour*, each by the late Frances Donaldson; Peters Fraser & Dunlop, agents for *Freddy Lonsdale* by the late Frances Donaldson; Longman Group Ltd, publishers of *A Quite Remarkable Father* by L R Howard; Faber and Faber Ltd, publishers of *The Bad Old Days* by Charles Graves; Agnes M Gautier, Co-Executor of the late Jimmy Heineman's literary interests, in respect of *Bolton and Wodehouse and Kern* by Lee Davis; HarperCollins Publishers Limited, publishers of *The Harold Nicolson Diaries 1939-45*, edited by Nigel Nicolson; Iain Sproat, author of *Wodehouse at War*; James Hogg, in respect of *Lord Emsworth's Annotated Whiffle* and Tams-Witmark Music Library, Inc, in respect of *Anything Goes*. Particular thanks go to Ms Robbin Reynolds for permission to quote extensively from letters by Paul R Reynolds Snr and Jnr, and to the Rare Book and Manuscript Library, Columbia University, the present owners of the Paul Revere Reynolds Papers.

The book contains quotations from a number of other sources. Sincere apologies are offered for those unsuccessful attempts which have been made to identify and contact the relevant publishers or copyrightholders. If contact is made by such persons with the publisher, such omission will be corrected gladly in any future edition of this work.

Three other friends have read virtually the full manuscript in draft and encouraged me to proceed: Chris Reece, editor of *Tax Journal*, who kindly published a series of four articles based on the book; Prof Evelyne d'Auzac, whose preliminary researches into the Reynolds Papers at Columbia University provided useful background information, and John Fletcher, prop' of Porpoise Books, the publisher. Barry Phelps saw part of an early draft and by a timely correction of a misunderstood fact saved me considerable time.

Tony Ring
July 1995

FOREWORD

Between 1909 and 1939, P G Wodehouse was a genuine intercontinental commuter, one of a small group of individuals whose chosen career meant that a considerable time was spent on transatlantic liners. In his case, it was principally the theatrical bug that caused the extensive travel, as his literary interests could largely have been handled from either the UK or the USA.

In the period before the second world war, transatlantic commuters were very much at the mercy of the world's revenue authorities. They were too rare a breed, and carried too few votes, for special tax laws to have been introduced to help their conservation, so it was quite the norm for income tax to be charged on the same income in both the country of residence of the earner, and the country from which the income was derived. And in some cases, in the country in which an individual was born as well! Since the concept of giving credits to reduce the incidence of double taxation was a post-war development, the overall tax bill could be penal.

It was a natural development for those affected to take advice on possible ways of reducing the burden of taxation. They were faced with two additional difficulties not present today. First, there was relatively little guidance on the interpretation of tax law from decided court cases, and secondly, there were relatively few competent practitioners, as both Wodehouse and Rafael Sabatini found to their considerable cost.

Wodehouse and his more able advisers were in the vanguard of those who sought to mitigate their cash tax liabilities. His view was that he was happy (well, perhaps not happy, but willing) to pay tax on his income once, but he didn't see why he should do so more than once. It did not really bother him which country collected, but it seemed logical that only one should.

His advisers assisted him variously in a number of tax planning devices:

a   use of a US corporation to reduce UK taxes,

b   use of a Swiss corporation to reduce UK taxes,

c   having him gift one-half of earnings from his future writings to his wife, to obtain the benefit of lower rates of US tax, and

d   becoming resident in France, a country which only taxed income derived from within its borders, thus ensuring only US tax was charged on US earnings, and only UK tax was charged on UK earnings.

All of these were effectively to become standard tax planning devices, either for authors, or international travellers, or both, although each to some degree broke new ground. The advisers also helped him challenge a few technical matters, such as whether the sale of US serial rights to a story should be regarded as generating royalty income or capital receipts.

Wodehouse's appearances in the Tax Courts covered a variety of these points, mostly permitting judicial consideration of matters where there was genuine uncertainty as to the proper meaning of the relevant law. There were, however, three disputes with potentially more damaging undertones, although an examination in detail of each shows that he was, in each instance, blameless.

The first of these, described in chapter 4, did not reach court. It arose from the blatant failure by John W Rumsey to fulfil his obligations in respect of a US corporation which he had incorporated, and was supposed to be managing, on Wodehouse's behalf. Once Wodehouse's other advisers had realised Rumsey's shortcomings, he was removed, but a series of avoidable delays by his advisers resulted in the discovery by the Internal Revenue Service (IRS) that the corporation's tax affairs were in arrears. The news of this development infuriated Wodehouse, who had already been pleading with his advisers to reach a settlement with the Revenue for more than a year.

The second and third allegations, described principally in chapter 7, had no substance, although a perfunctory glance would suggest they were of extreme seriousness. One was almost comic, a claim by the IRS in 1947 that Wodehouse had not filed his 1923 and 1924 tax returns in the USA. During the 1930s there had been a final settlement covering the period 1925 to 1933, and one might have thought that this tacitly cleared any earlier years. But no. During those two years Wodehouse regularly left the USA by liner, and would have been required to produce a "sailing permit" confirming that he was up-to-date with his tax obligations, and one might have thought that this would carry some weight. But no. When the matter came to court, the IRS refused to give any evidence acceptable to the judge about the extent of any search for the missing returns that they had undertaken. It is difficult for us, today, to see how the IRS thought they could win that case, and it is equally difficult to escape the conclusion that there was an element of bullying in the attack. Fortunately the allegation was brusquely thrown out of court.

The other allegation was on the face of it far more serious, but while it contained no element of comedy, there was, and remains, a feeling of utter disbelief that the IRS thought they had a case. They claimed that there was tax fraud in relation to the activities of the Swiss company which was used for a four year period from 1934 to 1937. Once again an occasional fact stood in the way of the bludgeon of the IRS. Fact one: the Swiss company had filed all its US tax returns on a timely basis. Fact two: the Swiss company had been audited by the IRS for its final trading period. Fact three: the IRS had been sufficiently satisfied with the company's tax returns that it had made a tax repayment in relation to the final trading period. Since tax fraud is generally accepted as requiring the existence of hidden information, or the presentation of misleading data to the Revenue, we cannot today understand their enthusiasm for the allegation. The court also found problems with it, and vigorously rejected their claim.

Despite his attempts to mitigate the burden of taxation, Wodehouse was very aware that to make any substantial savings, he would have to allow tax considerations to dictate his lifestyle to some degree, and he had to judge whether the financial saving was worth the personal inconvenience. His decisions were frequently in favour of the tax savings, so on many occasions he found himself effectively barred from visiting the UK (Leonora, William Townend, Dulwich College) until the beginning of the following tax year. But the most critical tax-related decision was to become a resident of France, which led directly to his being interned as a prisoner-of-war in 1940. The consequences are described in chapter 6, and shed a poor light on a number of Wodehouse's acquaintances, who were prepared to believe grossly inaccurate hearsay about alleged tax debts without waiting to be informed of any of the facts.

An important true story is thus explained comprehensively for the first time in this book, by an author whose professional career in the field of international taxation has enabled him to put the various facts into context, and show that any suggestion that Wodehouse sought to evade tax is wholly unjustified. The bare facts, which are extraordinary in themselves, are supported by Wodehouse's own correspondence, which forthrightly expresses his opinions of the tax system and the actions (or inaction) of some of his advisers, the frustration caused by the tax authorities and the tax system, and the numbing slowness with which any progress could be made. They demonstrate that, although in his early days he was too trusting in his assumption that his agents would do their job competently, Wodehouse at no stage acted improperly, but merely sought to mitigate legally the excessive burdens of an immature international tax system, using devices which subsequently became the industry norm.

Perhaps the only positive outcome from the trials and tribulations which he suffered at the hands of the tax authorities is reflected in by far the best writing in the book, the hundreds of extracts from the novels, stories, lyrics and essays in which Wodehouse felt it was necessary to make reference to his favourite, and almost only, enemy.

CHAPTER 1 — INTRODUCTION

Anyone who has read a range of Wodehouse novels or short stories will notice that a number of subjects crop up again and again, quite apart from the many similarities and repetitive aspects of plot, location and character. One will find frequent appearances by the clergy (always hoping to emerge intact from trying circumstances), by pet animals (of whom only Eustace the monkey really suffers to a material degree), by private detectives (always of doubtful moral outlook, and generally without recognisable professional ethics), by imposters, and by petty crooks whose sheer incompetence requires them to be regarded sympathetically by the reader, who guesses that they will rarely be able to keep or enjoy their ill-gotten gains — if they ever manage to getten them. And to be added to this list are the tax authorities, for Wodehouse makes regular sardonic references to income tax and death duties, to customs and excise duties, and to those who sell their soul by collecting them.

Norman Murphy, in his book *In Search of Blandings*[1] and from subsequent research, has confirmed beyond doubt what many suspected, that much of Wodehouse's writing was based on the exaggerated recollections of real people, places, incidents, news items and tangible objects. In the early days of his writing, before he had experienced at first hand their destructive potential as a source of trouble, he was able to treat taxes in a wholly light-hearted manner, as will be seen by the extracts in chapter 3. He did not overplay the subject — when it was used it was to amuse the reader but not to make any particular point. It reflected the mood of the time — that the tax authorities were fair game as a butt of humour; no one really liked paying taxes but accepted that governments had to raise money somehow! In later works, the comments that his characters express about taxes represent a personal depth of feeling even greater than the natural antipathy which is familiar to us all, when asked to dig deep into our pockets to meet the demands of some nameless bureaucrat, or worse, an impersonal, error-strewn, computer.

1

From 1923 to 1950, Wodehouse was in dispute with a country's tax authorities, had just settled a dispute, was about to become involved in a dispute, or was being unfairly pilloried in public because of a past dispute. As explained in the Foreword, this circumstance did not derive from any deliberate attempt to evade his obligations. In reality, tax laws at the time were essentially designed to meet the requirements of domestic rather than international circumstances, and the international commuter was exposed to extremely pernicious double taxation. Wodehouse and his contemporaries were advised to take certain steps to legally reduce the tax burden. This could not be achieved without personal cost — one of the consequences for the Wodehouses was reduced flexibility in their choice of place to live from time to time. In view of the frustration which this caused, coupled with the fact — as will be shown as the plot of this story unfolds — that he was generally much more in the right than in the wrong, it is hardly surprising that he took and expressed a jaundiced view about the activities of the revenue authorities.

The subject of taxes is one which is so emotive, and so dear to all our hearts, that a study of its impact on the life of one of the world's best-loved writers should offer plenty of scope for anger, humour, irony and sheer disbelief. It is, for example, ironic but certain that the combined incidence of UK and US taxes — and the brushes he had already had with the authorities in each country — was a major, if not *the* major, reason why he was living in France at the outbreak of the second world war, one of the consequences of which was that he never visited the UK again.

Readers may care to digest most of this book as a series of two-course meals. Although it contains occasional traps for the unwary — like a good golf course — each chapter from the third onwards divides naturally into an entrée (substantial, with many complex ingredients) and a dessert (which Uncle Tom would surely appreciate as one of Anatole's lightest soufflés). It is to be hoped that readers who manage to negotiate the whole of this book will have been able to identify the cause of the frustration and anger that Wodehouse must have felt, and to admire the humour with which, as usual, he clothed it.

2

Perhaps a friendly warning should be given to readers that some of the more difficult bunkers and sand-traps which have to be negotiated have been built on the secondary course, the Appendix, as the nature of this book makes it inevitable that there is some detailed technical analysis and commentary of the legal aspects of Wodehouse's tax position. One approach that Wodehouse took in starting some of his later books was to explain how difficult it was to retain the interest of the familiar reader whilst giving the newcomer sufficient background to enable him or her to pick up the nuances of the following 200 pages (see, for example, **Much Obliged, Jeeves**[2]). In this book the problem has been tackled by including in chapter 2 sufficient material to provide a superficial awareness, and then to expand both technical detail and commentary in the Appendix. By this means, it is to be hoped that readers who, for some inexplicable reason, wish to stay in complete ignorance of the rules relating to the interaction of the UK and US systems of personal taxation at the stage of development which they had reached in the 1920s and 1930s, will not be dissuaded from reaching the fascinating story unveiled from chapter 3 onwards.

And so to the structure of the book. As a further introduction, an attempt to put Wodehouse's actions into perspective, the views of a small number of his contemporaries about the scheme of taxation which they faced, which was very different to that which is operative today, have been brought together. And this has been linked with a brief discussion of the ethical, or moral, aspects of attempting to save tax.

The context having been set, Wodehouse's detailed tax history then divides fairly naturally into six eons, as described below. Of course, there is a seventh, following his death in 1975, during which the inevitable complexities of settling the tax position of an international estate could be seen at their most testing. That story, alas, is only for the eyes of the Trustees and Executors, and will remain forever unpublished. One might assume that an observant spectator looking down from above would relish the prospect of finding some new and sarcastic comments to make about the tax gatherers, especially those involved with estate or death duties. But for those we will have to await the Complete Ethereal Wodehouse, for copyright reasons available only to those resident in Heaven.

The break-points which have been selected are:

1   to 1923, when a settlement was reached following discussions about his status in the United States for filing tax returns, and the extent to which he was liable to pay tax there,

2   to 1931, a stable period, during which the authorities were merely filling eelskins preparatory to hitting him over the head, but during which there were no recorded actual skirmishes,

3   to 1936, when in Wodehouse's own words, "Hell's foundations were quivering". He and his advisers were involved in a dispute in the US which covered the period from 1925 to 1931, and such was the aggression of the Revenue authorities that not only did they demand over $ 250,000 from him, but they put a lien on funds due from US sources, which meant that he could effectively not draw money in the United States. And to add to the fun, the UK Revenue decided to assess him to increased UK taxes as well. This period undoubtedly represented one of the highspots in terms of his relations with the tax authorities, and in theatrical terms was equivalent to the end of Act I,

4   to 1943, when as a result of the double burden of taxation in England and the USA, the Wodehouses had chosen to live in France, only to still be there at the outbreak of war. The latter half of this period featured self-righteous but wholly inaccurate and almost deliberately misleading correspondence in the press concerning Wodehouse's alleged tax debts,

5   to 1950, when the crass ineptitude of the US tax-gathering system, with its ability to maximise cost, worry and bureaucracy, and minimise logic, was to be seen at its peak with a trip to Cloud-cuckoo-land, and inconsistent solutions being found for a series of technical disputes, the overall effect of which was to cock a large snook at the wartime correspondents, and

6   to 1975, during which period it seems that the daily routines of working for the Revenue services were handled with sufficient assiduity to satisfy even the most tenacious Revenue investigator. At least there were no more disputes sufficiently serious to land up in court.

It is into these distinct periods that the bulk of the book is divided. In respect of each, its chapter covers first the substance of any disputes, then the correspondence and other contemporary references to Wodehouse's attitude at the time, and finally the Wodehouse writings of the period in which taxation was mentioned. The correlation between his treatment by the tax authorities and his increasingly irreverent treatment of the tax authorities is there for all to see. If anything is surprising, it is to observe quite how gently he treated them. But then, if Wodehouse had a philosophy, it was to implore his readers not to allow themselves to stay serious for more than half an hour at a time, and to urge them not to hurt another's feelings unduly. He seems to have followed this philosophy in his own life — he is always spoken of as a gentle man, with no bitterness, and the placid humour he invokes to gently tease the revenue is in this vein.

Footnotes

1 1981 (Private); 1986 (Salem House)
2 1971 (Barrie & Jenkins)

CHAPTER 2 — IS TAX AVOIDANCE CULPABLE?

In this chapter, the following questions are addressed:

What was Wodehouse seeking to do when he took the advice of professional advisers to seek to minimise his taxes?

And was what he was trying to do legal?

Even today, when tax rates have fallen from their ludicrous peaks of the 1960s and 1970s (when in the UK they reached 98% and in one notorious year income from investments was actually taxed at a rate in excess of 100%), there is no general agreement as to what constitutes, morally or ethically, acceptable tax avoidance, ie the attempt to reduce legally the incidence of taxation.

In the UK, the starting point is generally taken as a series of comments made by Judges in the course of various tax cases heard in the courts between the wars. Lord Sumner said in the 1926 case *Inland Revenue Commissioners (IRC) v Fisher's Executors*:

> "My Lords, the highest authorities have always recognised that the subject is entitled so to arrange his affairs as not to attract taxes imposed by the Crown, so far as he can do so within the law, and that he may legitimately claim the advantage of any express term or of any omissions that he can find in his favour in the taxing Acts. In so doing, he neither comes under liability nor incurs blame."

This was followed, in 1929, in the case *Ayrshire Pullman Motor Services and Ritchie v IRC*, by the dicta of Lord Clyde:

> "No man in this country is under the smallest obligation, moral or other, so to arrange his legal relations to his business or to his property as to enable the Inland Revenue to put the largest possible shovel into his stores...The taxpayer is...entitled to be astute to prevent, so far as he honestly can, the depletion of his means by the Inland Revenue."

And then, in 1936, the position was restated by Lord Tomlin in the House of Lords in *IRC v Duke of Westminster*, in these words:

> "Every man is entitled if he can to order his affairs so as that the tax attracted under the appropriate Act is less than it otherwise would be. If he succeeds in ordering them so as to secure this result, then however unappreciative the Commissioners of Inland Revenue or his fellow taxpayers may be of his ingenuity, he cannot be compelled to pay an increased tax."

So it is clear that the possibility of saving taxes — which Wodehouse and his advisers must have had in mind when he entered into the various changes in his business arrangements — would not have met with resistance in the UK provided they met the technical requirements of the UK tax laws. (It is true that the attitudes of the UK Courts have hardened to some extent since those heady inter-war days, but only since Wodehouse's death.)

There is indicative evidence that an attempt is being made to reach some sort of consensus between advisers and the authorities in the UK as to what should be regarded as "tax avoidance", and thus vulnerable to attack by the authorities, as compared to "tax mitigation", about which they should raise no eyebrows. This has evolved during an investigation by the Government's National Audit Office into ways of preventing tax avoidance in relation to the UK's form of sales tax, Value Added Tax. In the consultations with professional bodies, *The Institute of Taxation* (now the Chartered Institute of Taxation), the leading body representing tax practitioners, proposed a broad indication of the characteristics of tax avoidance, ie of transactions which, while legal, were a fair target for the authorities to attack, either by new legislation, or through the courts.

In this context, "tax avoidance" was to be distinguished from both "tax mitigation" and "tax evasion". The criteria which distinguished tax avoidance, which were accepted by H M Customs and Excise as representing working guidelines, refer to arrangements which:

*   are by their nature designed to avoid or
     reduce liability to tax;

*   are brought into existence solely with that
     end in mind and not with a view to achieving
     some other commercial purpose of the
     business, even though they might be carried
     out in an overall commercial context; and

*   can be recognised (even if not described in
     advance) as outside the broad intention of
     the tax legislation.

Readers may wish to test Wodehouse's actions against these
criteria to help them decide whether he was stepping across the
bounds of what the ordinary person might today consider
reasonable. But while doing so, it is important to realise that
transactions which fulfil these criteria even today remain legal in
the UK. Their ability to achieve their tax-saving objective depends
on how efficiently they were carried out, and how their overall
consequences are viewed by the Courts.

So it has to be realised that there is, and perhaps always has
been, a white line, on one side of which one could take all sorts
of legal steps which even tax authorities would not seek to
counteract ("tax mitigation"). A law may have been enacted
specifically to provide a tax saving (eg a deduction from taxable
income for interest paid) or to provide an incentive to save in a
way which provides tax-free income, so avoidance of tax can in
some cases be a deliberate part of government policy. There are
numerous examples of laws, or parts of laws, which deliberately
provide such a tax saving. No-one could, for example, criticise
Wodehouse or any other individual for claiming the personal
deduction available to any US individual taxpayer. In the same
way, no-one would criticise a small businessman for claiming
depreciation of business assets at accelerated rates — as they are
urged to do by the government. Professional tax advisers are
surely not to be pilloried if they draw to their clients' attention the
fact that certain tax-free bonds may from time to time provide a

higher interest return net of tax than other instruments where the nominally higher interest rate is subject to tax. These examples are clearly generally acceptable, and all fall within the concept of mitigation.

But there is another line, perhaps black, on the far side of which one finds the clearly illegal acts which constitute tax evasion — fraud through non-disclosure, misrepresentation, etc. Professional tax advisers will have no truck with that wasteland, and nor did Wodehouse. He seemed to have been aware of the distinction between tax avoidance and tax evasion, and he rarely fell into the trap of referring in writing to evasion[1]. One can find one or two suggestions in his correspondence which, if pursued, might have been illegal, but wiser counsels seem to have prevailed as there is no evidence that they were any more than figments of the imagination born from frustration.

Between the two lines is a vast area of greyness, which can be described as tax avoidance, some patches of which are darker than others, for this area encompasses not only transactions to which only a purist, arguing that a person should not do anything deliberately to reduce his share of the communal burdens, might object, but also the artificial schemes, marketed by impersonal technicians, which are within the *Institute of Taxation* criteria on tax avoidance.

Typically, many of these schemes not only have no commercial merit or effect whatsoever — apart perhaps from the arrangement fee paid — but depend for their viability on the cumulative tax saving achieved by undertaking certain paper transactions in a particular order. As already stated, these transactions will each be perfectly legal in principle, but two questions have to be addressed: are they effective for tax purposes, and are the circumstances (and all relevant documents) FULLY disclosed to the tax authorities?

Some advisers are prepared to stand firmly behind their view that the steps are effective, and will seek to disguise or simply not disclose the full story because they believe the Revenue have no reason to challenge the transaction(s) in question. That approach can validly be considered unacceptable and indeed may be professionally unethical. But if an adviser and taxpayer undertake the same actions, fully disclose the circumstances to the authorities, and challenge them to prove they are not effective, that represents the proper working of democracy. Taxpayers, or their advisers, may, in practice, be ostracised if their peers consider their actions morally indefensible, but there can be no question of illegality in those circumstances. Ineffectiveness must always be distinguished from illegality. This principle should apply equally in both the UK and the US, despite the very different approach taken by the revenue authorities in the two countries to audit and verification.

As part of their campaign to have transactions with little commercial merit treated as ineffective for tax purposes, the US Revenue authorities invented the concept of the "sham" transaction, (not dissimilar to the second of the criteria listed above), which they say has no effect. This, they consider, entitles them to seek to nullify any tax benefits perceived to be derived from the transaction. If the Revenue can establish through the Courts that in any particular dispute their views in any case are right, then for that dispute, they can claim game, set and match.

But that should not stop other taxpayers who so wish from continuing to try to arrange their affairs so as to minimise their tax bills, free from any concern that they will be unfairly treated by the tax authorities. There are undoubtedly public-spirited taxpayers who do not take steps they are entitled to in order to reduce taxes, either from reasons of personal conscience, laziness, ignorance or lack of sound professional advice. But should that prevent the remainder from pursuing a policy of seeking to minimise their taxes? And is there a moral point beyond which a taxpayer should not go, or beyond which a professional adviser should not advise? If there is, how does it change over time, so that we do not judge events of sixty years ago by today's standards?

In looking at these questions from Wodehouse's point of view, perhaps the most important differences in the inter-war period from today are:

1 the lack of sophistication in the commercial and tax law, particularly in respect of international taxation. In the UK alone, over 2,000 pages of new tax legislation were enacted in the 1980's, and twice as much information of equal relevance such as statements of Revenue practice, statutory regulations and the decisions of courts and tribunals needed to be studied by taxpayers and their advisers.

2 the lack of skilled tax advisers. Because they were relatively few in number, there was less scope for informed debate on the precise meanings of various pieces of legislation.

3 the lack of precedent in the form of case hearings during which points had previously been debated in the Courts. For example, some of the points in the Wodehouse litigation were decided by reference to the Rafael Sabatini and Sax Rohmer cases. The latter two were only heard in 1938 and 1946 respectively, so it was impossible for the correct, approved, interpretation of the relevant matters to have been known by Wodehouse's advisers in the mid-1930's, the period during which actions were taken which were to create the background for his cases. And even then, the Courts occasionally overturn earlier decisions which have been regarded as the cornerstone of the law, sometimes in the taxpayer's favour. In November 1992, for example, the House of Lords (UK Supreme Court) overturned a precedent of some 250 years to enable the taxpayer to succeed in the case of *Pepper v Hart*.

11

4 Even when a point of law had been considered by the courts, there might be different decisions on similar facts. On two of the points which Wodehouse took to the Appeal Courts in the US, different Circuits came up with diametrically opposed answers! And it was not the case of one court being pro-taxpayer on both issues, as the Wodehouse victories were in different districts! In those circumstances, how could any taxpayer know on what interpretation of the law he or she should file subsequent years' tax returns?

5 Wodehouse's circumstances, while not unique, were sufficiently unusual not to have required the specific attention of the US legislature. No one had given adequate thought to the many problems which arose for an international commuter, not a citizen of (and maybe not even resident in) the US, who was working on such a wide range of projects as he was. No one wondered whether the burdens he might have had to bear if he had taken no steps to reduce his taxes would be fair. Some of his comments about his peers (for example pages 21-22) are good illustrations of his genuine concerns for the impact of the system in general.

When you add to these points the fact that both the Wodehouses had an eye for the doubloons, especially after the losses incurred in the Wall Street Crash in 1929, it is understandable why he was not shy in accepting suggestions from advisers as to ways in which he could legitimately reduce his tax bill. From his earliest days as a writer, he had demonstrated his awareness of the humorous potential of the demon taxation (see for example **William Tell Told Again**, chapter 3). By the end of the 1920s he was earning enough to make it worthwhile to consider putting into practice some of the ideas for taming the demon about which he had heard.

It is interesting to read in Paul R Reynolds' book, **The Middle Man**[2], that he as literary agent was on the look out for ways to help his clients reduce their taxes, as this extract shows:

Luck played a part for me with [representing] another fantastic writer and historian.

William L Shirer was an outstanding radio news broadcaster and commentator in Berlin during the first two years of the Second World War. The entry of the United States into the war forced Shirer to leave Germany. Back in the US he wrote **Berlin Diary** which had an enormous sale.

Shirer, stationed in the United States, resumed broadcasting for CBS and later from Mutual. Then during the McCarthy era he was smeared as a Red and thrown off the air. There was no basis for the smear. Shirer was liberal in his outlook but not a Communist nor a pink nor a fellow traveler in any rational use of those words. The smear ended Shirer's radio career. His luck seemed abominable.

Shirer, who resumed writing books, was unhappy with his agent. Most of the royalties earned by **Berlin Diary** had been paid in one year. This put Shirer into a high income tax bracket and left him with relatively little actual money. What happened to Shirer happened to Richard Wright with his best seller, **Native Son**, which I represented. This book made thousands and thousands of dollars, most of which was paid in one year, and a large percentage of Wright's earnings went to Uncle Sam.

Thinking about the Wright situation it occurred to me that it should be possible to draw a contract with a publisher whereby the publisher was limited as to the amount of money he could pay an author in any one year. By spreading the author's royalties over a period of years the author would be kept out of the very high income tax brackets in any one tax year. I consulted two different well-known law firms as to the legality of such a contract. Lawyers are rarely helpful and the opinions given me were not definite. Both firms said the courts might sustain such a contract and might not. Believing that authors had nothing to lose and possibly much to gain, I drew the contracts for Wright's next best seller, **Black Boy**, and for the Shellaberger novels starting with **Captain from Castile**, spreading the money over a number of years. No income tax troubles occurred. Ultimately the Internal Revenue gave its formal blessing to this practice. Today [1972] spreading of an author's income over a period of years is almost universal.

It is reasonable to assume that some form of spreading of income for authors is either provided in the tax law of most Western countries, or can be achieved by well-known devices such as a version of the contract described by Reynolds.

As explained above, tax professionals will always distinguish between tax evasion — which relies for its efficacy on some illegal aspect such as fraud, deliberately providing false information or otherwise not paying one's full taxes due under the law — and tax avoidance or mitigation, which means reducing one's tax bill by arranging one's affairs in a particular way so the attempt of the legislature to skin one to the bone is defeated. But even tax professionals will not always agree whether some of the dark grey patches referred to above should really be regarded as evasion.

Another point which the reader should bear in mind when reading some of the comments made in public about the Wodehouse tax experience is that, contrary to the apparent belief of the commentators, the mere fact that tax was assessed by Revenue authorities had no bearing on whether it was actually payable! The Revenue, for their sins, are responsible to governments for making assessments to the best of their judgment by applying their interpretation of the law to the facts in their possession, and for making estimates of tax liabilities if they are not given adequate facts. Now if there are two sides to a dispute, for each lawyer who is right there must be one who is wrong, so in a considerable number of cases the Revenue will be wrong in their interpretation of the law. Except indirectly in the case of Jeeves Dramatics, Inc (see chapter 4), Wodehouse had not failed to provide the necessary information — the problem was that his advisers disagreed with the interpretation of the law preferred by the Revenue. The Revenue could not pursue their view without raising tax assessments which could be tested in Court, so the assessments were issued. But it is totally erroneous to suggest, as did some self-publicists, that these amounts were <u>owed</u> by Wodehouse. It might have been what the Revenue thought he owed, but the debate had yet to begin.

It comes as no surprise that there is a lot of confusion in the minds of the public about what tax liabilities really are, when they arise and whether it is legitimate to take certain steps which may reduce the amount of tax to be paid. And Wodehouse — amongst others — has suffered from each of these misunderstandings.

Except where people choose to misunderstand the true nuances of the term tax evasion — as for their personal or unprofessional reasons certain politicians, journalists, tax collectors and smug critics are from time to time deliberately prone to do — real difficulties only arise in practice when a taxpayer does something he or she honestly believes is within the law, but that conclusion turns out to be wrong. In that case the culpability (and attributing to the transaction the correct label as evasion or avoidance) depends on a court's subjective judgment of whether reasonable care was taken by the taxpayer and his advisers. The more professional advice that was taken, and the greater the uncertainty inherent in the law itself, the less likely it is that a transaction should be tainted as deliberate tax evasion.

The question of the morality of tax avoidance is not really distinguishable from similar questions about a whole range of other matters where there is the opportunity for an individual to take steps, which some would consider selfish, to benefit oneself or one's family at the apparent expense of the community. If the steps taken are themselves legal, any judgment becomes merely a moral one, and one should not seek to attribute more sinister motives.

15

This point can be illustrated with an example from the late Lady Frances Donaldson's autobiography, *A Twentieth-Century Life*[3], which must be representative of the attitude adopted by thousands of others at the time. She noted in her diary on 13 March, 1941, that:

> Ernest Bevin has just announced the conscription of women, beginning with the 20's and 21's. This won't affect me, as I am both a mother and a farmer. But I am wondering if it may eventually affect either Molly [Hands, a private teacher/nanny to her children] or Nora [presumably, Leonora Wodehouse]. I am going to make Molly do a lot of farm work all summer, so as to be able to call her a part-time farm worker.

No doubt very understandable motives! The 1941 rules for conscripting women were doubtless complex, apparently loosely drafted, and one is in no position to offer any sort of judgment. But is this not comparable to the question of tax avoidance? The object was to obtain a "selfish" advantage (the continued service and/or safety of a friend/employee) at the expense of the community (the strengthening of the country's armed forces at a time of war). *IF* the steps mentioned were actually taken and met the objectives — and one can confidently assume in this case that they were and did — then the action was legal and cannot be attacked other than on moral grounds. And an attack on this type of avoidance — the avoidance of conscription — would be every bit as subjective as an attack on legal tax avoidance. Or to put it another way, an attack on legal tax avoidance would be every bit as subjective as an attack on the avoidance of conscription. And at a time of war, a topic every bit as likely to be affected by emotion.

One can thus ask, if Wodehouse deserved to be condemned for his attempts to save taxes, did Lady Donaldson, and did the tens of thousands of others who took similar steps, deserve to be condemned equally for the actions they took or proposed to take to help another to avoid conscription?

In the following chapters, as the nature of what Wodehouse was trying to achieve becomes clearer, readers will be drawn inexorably to the conclusion that he and his advisers were engaged in a number of steps representing little, if anything, more than acceptable tax avoidance of the type which became commonplace during the subsequent fifty years. There are even those who would say that, had his advisers not suggested that the steps be taken, they would have been guilty of negligence to their client. (Such a charge may not have stuck in the 1930s, but one would be less sanguine about the defendant's chances in the litigious 1990s!) And one is entitled to ask whether, if anything other than attempts to save taxes through legal avoidance were in point, Wodehouse would have been so determined to take the case all the way through the US courts, knowing the reports of the court proceedings would be exposed to the public gaze.

Like Wodehouse, Sir Alan Herbert was involved in a long-running battle with the authorities on the question of taxation, in his case lasting more than forty years. He was not fighting in relation to his personal affairs, but was supporting the attempts being made to remove a "temporary" tax on various forms of entertainment (but not books) which had been imposed (along with duties on matches, cider, perry, soda-syphons and rail fares over 9d) in 1916 along with a promise that it would be abolished as soon as the first world war was over!

As an MP, he was able to have direct access to many ministers and civil servants, to whom he pleaded the cause, and of course was able to put his point of view directly to Parliament. He described the hypocrisy of various governments and Chancellors of the Exchequer in an entertaining book entitled *No Fine on Fun*[4], pointing out that Parliament tinkered with the tax, sometimes making it more onerous, sometimes less, more than 20 times in the 40 years about which he wrote, but despite numerous promises it never was abolished. And even today (1995), when value added tax is still not charged on books, there is a 17½% VAT on tickets to the live theatre. If he were starting his campaign today, Sir Alan would surely adopt a twin-pronged approach — try to have the law changed, but at the same time

17

seek loopholes in the text of the legislation which might offer an opportunity to reduce the amount of tax which had to be paid within the rules.

The entertainment tax was a petty tax, with relatively little money-raising capability. Despite those twenty alterations to the law in forty years, there remained numerous uncertainties as to how the tax applied in certain circumstances. Taxes on income raised far more revenue, and the rules by which they operated were far more complex. Wodehouse had no champion in the UK Parliament or the US Congress. If the rules on entertainment tax could not be altered by a group of MPs who were passionately interested in its abolition, what hope could he seriously have had of expecting a change in the rules relating to penal double taxation of income in the UK and US. Self-help through legal tax mitigation starts to appear more rational and legitimate than ever.

There is some circumstantial evidence that in the 1910s and even in the 1920s Wodehouse (and more particularly his advisers) may have paid inadequate attention to the timely filing of necessary tax returns, but the rules then were so different, and information about that period so sparse, that it is difficult to reach any firm conclusions. And even if this were the case, the delays occurred in relation to the US tax returns of his US company Jeeves Dramatics, Inc, for the administration of which one of his advisers had stated his specific responsibility in writing. In addition, one must not overlook the fact that the US had a much more formalised system of tax administration than that subsisting in the UK with which Wodehouse grew up and which enjoyed much more flexible deadlines. Even today, if a British resident receives a tax return on April 6, with a statement that he is required to return it completed within 30 days, he will bear no penalties if he files it by October 31. And this represents a significant tightening of the rules over the last five years!

So, what did Wodehouse's peers think about the tax regimes under which they toiled? The following extracts from various sources give a flavour in support of the comments already made:

Harold Nicolson (British author and socialist politician, married to Vita Sackville-West), 1932[5]:

We have about £ 1,000 owing from America. We do not want to use it because of income tax.

From Bill Townend, an added comment in **Performing Flea**[6], *published in 1953, about Billy Rose:*

The Billy Rose whom Plum mentions as his collaborator in the lyrics of the Chinese musical play shortly afterwards [1929] became a millionaire. During the great fair, he ran what was called the Aquacade, a swimming-and-diving-belle entertainment out near La Guardia airfield. His expenses per week were thirty thousand dollars, and he never failed to take in a hundred thousand, one bumper week topping two hundred and sixty thousand. This went on all through the summer, and it was at a time when the American income tax was a mere nineteen per cent.

Frances Donaldson (British author of a number of biographies, including those of PGW and Evelyn Waugh), writing about the author Daphne du Maurier[7]:

She came back into my life because of a passage in my book **Evelyn Waugh: Portrait of a Country Neighbour**[8]. Evelyn was at the time obsessed by the income tax he had to pay and in my book I quoted the following letter he wrote to me to prove it was impossible for a writer to earn more than a limited annual income, even allowing for certain concessions:

19

8 May 1954

Lady Browning (ie du Maurier) income:
100,000 @ 12/6, 20% royalty = £ 12,500.
At 150,000, £ 6,250 increase.

Full rates of taxation £ 6,250 = c £ 156.

[Author's comment — UK tax rates at the time could reach 19/6d in the £ even for earned income]

I had chosen D du M in conversation as one of the few writers who hit the jackpot with every book. The meaning of Evelyn's letter may not be entirely clear, nor the facts completely accurate. But the point is, while on all his earnings the writer paid tax and supertax he could neither by hard work nor unusual success raise these earnings in good years to save against bad.

When my book appeared in 1967 I received a long letter from Daphne in which she said "I was so amused at the reference and how right Evelyn Waugh was about my Income Tax."

Letter from Evelyn Waugh to Wodehouse in 1957[9], commenting wryly on a source of income which remained tax-free, and linking nicely with the preceding extract:

The verdict last week [in an action against Nancy Spain, a journalist with the **Daily Express**] was a great surprise and delight to me. The action was merely a preliminary skirmish before a larger battle which, in accordance with your sage advice, I am joining with the Express. The second libel is altogether graver, and I hope will be remunerative. Damages for libel are the only tax-free earnings possible now.

Letter from Sax Rohmer[10], author of the Fu Manchu tales, as part of the correspondence on the PGW wartime controversy:

Mr W A Darlington's reference to a claim for £ 50,000 made by the United States Revenue upon P G Wodehouse is calculated to mislead ... I would like to point out that a similar claim (in my own case for a less staggering sum) was made on all English novelists and playrights, or all of those with whom I am acquainted, who derived any considerable revenue from the U.S.A.

These claims are based upon some obscure paragraph in the statute book hitherto overlooked even by the lawyers. Nevertheless assessment was made retrospective. Rafael Sabatini heroically took the matter to court and fought a losing action which dragged on for more than a year.

In fairness to a man whose good name is at stake on other counts, I think the implication that Wodehouse's misfortune was due to conscious tax-dodging should be disclaimed.

Letter written by PGW himself from Hollywood to Bill Townend[11], giving some hearsay evidence about the position of his peers:

The taxes are fantastic here and very tough on Hollywood stars because they make so much over a short period and then go into the discard. Nelson Eddy, my neighbour,

made $ 600,000 last year, and when all his
taxes and expenses were paid found that he
had $ 50,000 left. Well, not bad, even so,
one might say. But then the point is that in
1939 his income may be about tuppence!
Stars shoot up and die away here before you
can breathe.

It is evident from the above that other authors had their problems
also. The British author Hugh Walpole was amongst them, and
the following extracts from his biography by Rupert Hart-Davis[12]
show how he not only got into serious tax arrears, but failed to
take his plight seriously for far too long. And readers can see from
the year to which each quotation relates, that his problem recurred
over a substantial part of his writing career:

1915

Meanwhile the delighted author spent a long week-end
at Polperro, followed by a few crowded days in London,
during which he visited a tax-collector and "settled with
him for £ 21" — *O sic semper!*

1922

Three days in London were quite enough, since they
included a "horrible morning with the accountant over
the income-tax papers, and I shall never forget it. I may
have to pay thousands of pounds. The only thing to do
is to Coué myself and to refuse to allow it to worry
me." All through the years he carried out this policy: he
kept no accounts, and as earnings from journalism,
films, lectures, and serials swelled the flow of royalties
from books, the precept of Dr Coué was merged into
the example of the ostrich. Considering how much he
allowed his periodical sessions with chartered
accountants and tax-inspectors to worry him — quite
unnecessarily — for his earning-power was always
greater — it is astonishing that he never took conclusive

steps to clear the matter up. He enjoyed nursing the illusion that all his affairs were in perfect order, but after his death his executors were obliged to negotiate for several years before the authorities finally agreed to accept the sum of £ 10,000 in settlement of the *arrears* of income tax and surtax.

1936

As the time of departure [from US] drew near, he became daily more nervous and wrought up. Not without cause, for two days before he was due to leave, *Kim* was still unfinished, his American income tax was unsettled, and ......

Eventually, everything was settled — or, as in the matter of the income tax, shelved — and on June 5 Hugh, with Harold at his side, took his last farewell of Hollywood.

[Author's note — it was still necessary at this time for those departing from the US to demonstrate that they did not owe any US income tax by submitting what was called, and euphemistically still is, a sailing permit. Readers are invited to remember this point in particular when reading chapters 6 and 7.]

1936

Towards the end of March he confessed in his journal that most of his film earnings had been spent (without, although he omitted this vital fact, any allowance for income tax) on pictures and books.

1937

The end of January was further darkened by another of his unending struggles with the tax authorities. As has been seen, Hugh kept no regular accounts, his memory of such matters was faulty, his arithmetic and his carelessness appalling (once he accidentally made out a cheque for more than a million pounds), and his income arrived at odd intervals from so many different sources that his advisers were always struggling to keep pace. Until his second long sojourn in Hollywood all had gone comparatively smoothly, but during those nine months his tax position became entangled in a heart-breaking snarl which was not finally unravelled until some years after his death. Periodical discussions with chartered accountants became regular annoyances to him, and almost every year he was obliged to sell some shares in order to satisfy the Inland Revenue. At one particularly black moment he rallied himself by reflecting that "my big income tax does mean I'm helping the country a bit".

1940

A heavy cold, threatening the pneumonia so dreaded by diabetics, kept him miserably in bed for a week; nor was his recovery helped by a visit from his income-tax adviser, who had just discovered a further £ 4,000 of untaxed income dating back to 1938.

1940/41

At the end of [January] he received a "letter from Inland Revenue saying I've paid no taxes since 1936! Some error here."

In an article *Reading For Love*[13], Walpole described his love for books and libraries, and makes the point that you cannot read all the books in a library simultaneously. He then adds:

Two or three books *can* be read at the same time, than which there is nothing pleasanter; a taste of Sir Thomas Brown in the morning, Jane Austen for tea and Peacock for supper — could anything be pleasanter? The trouble about one's duty to one's library springs rather from one's state of mind. A sudden wave of conscience at the cheating of the Chancellor of the Exchequer over income-tax may lead one to the sermons of Hooker and John Wesley's *Journal*, and it is then that your Congreves and Wycherlys and fine paper editions of Petronius with illustrations will feel themselves outrageously neglected.

Walpole's periodic tax problems, unresolved even as late as 1940/41, were not, in retrospect, surprising. We are not told that he took specific steps to reduce his liability by legitimate planning; his difficulties appear to have stemmed more from dilatoriness, almost certainly a deliberate dilatoriness born from a philosophy of laissez-faire.

Mention has been made twice in this chapter of the late Lady Donaldson, and it is to her that the last extracts from biographies in this chapter can be credited. In 1957 she produced a biography of her playwright father entitled simply **Freddy Lonsdale**[14], and observed in a number of places that he also had concerns about taxation. She put forward the following explanation of her father's apparently perpetual travelling:

> ...I think it was the occupational disease of the successful writer at its most advanced. When a writer is a young man, and before he has achieved success, he usually marries, because, more than anyone else in the world, he needs the faith in his power and the encouragement which only a wife can give. Then, like any normal person, he has some children. Often many years pass while life is simply a struggle to maintain this family. Then success comes, and with it, or so it was in the days before the level of income tax prevented this, comes an unexpectedly large income. All men find it necessary at times to assert their independence, but the writer is upheld in this desire by the belief that only by moving out into the world can he find the raw material for his trade....

Freddy Lonsdale seems to have left most of his financial affairs in the hands of Miss Cheshire, who was absolutely loyal to her interests. She arranged to bank much of his income in her name, and, later in his life, when enormous sums had to be found for income tax or one of his family, Miss Chester would produce the fees of some past production and with a wave of her wand make the problem disappear. Although Wodehouse had a similar assistant to look after his UK finances, Miss Matusch, she does not seem to have played quite such a prominent role in his affairs as Miss Cheshire did with Freddy Lonsdale.

Lonsdale lived to as a high a standard as he could at any time, or quite conceivably beyond. That was not unusual for the artistic community in those days, but it did cause Frances Donaldson to say, while writing about the 1930s:

> One of the things I have always found it difficult to explain is, given that he did not keep yachts or racehorses or gamble on the Stock Exchange, how he managed to get through the enormous sums he had earned in all these years in what seems now such a comparatively short space of time. He had, it is true, expenses which, given the present level* of income tax, no writer could nowadays sustain....It is apparent that he spent in unnecessary travel the equivalent of several thousand pounds a year.   "

* [Author's note — in the UK in 1957, the tax rate on earnings over £ 10,000 was in excess of 90%]

And she returned to this subject when writing about the 1950s:

> [Freddy] was extremely worried about money. I have recorded elsewhere that he had a diminishing capital sum on which he was living, and that he knew quite well that, whether or not he had the ability to earn new money, too much of it, if earned, would nowadays go in income tax for him to be able to afford the millionaire's life he was accustomed to.

Harold Nicolson, Evelyn Waugh, Hugh Walpole, Freddy Lonsdale, Nelson Eddy. The list is impressive, and other authors, such as E Phillips Oppenheim, Rafael Sabatini, Sax Rohmer and Guy Bolton will play their part as the drama unfolds. Wodehouse may have blazed some trails by his actions, but his was not a unique position. Each author had his own adviser; each adviser took a slightly different approach; each client responded with a different degree of enthusiasm to the suggestions that might have been made. Wodehouse's adventures with the taxman, like others in his life, have been more misrepresented than most, and it is to be hoped that the remainder of this work will put the record straight.

Footnotes

1 But see, for example, pages 30, 114
2 1972, William Morris, NY
3 1992, Weidenfeld & Nicholson
4 1957, Methuen
5 Diaries and Letters 1930-1964. 1980, Collins
6 1953, Herbert Jenkins
7 1992, Weidenfeld & Nicholson
8 1967, Weidenfeld & Nicholson
9 Modern and Literary Manuscripts, British Library
10 July 7, 1941, Daily Telegraph
11 Performing Flea. 1953, Herbert Jenkins
12 Hugh Walpole. 1952, Macmillan
13 November 1926, Strand
14 1957, Heinemann

CHAPTER 3: 1902 to 1923 — LEARNING
ALL ABOUT THE INCOME TAX

Partly because there were no serious disputes concerning tax in the first twenty years or so of his writing career, very little is known about Wodehouse's tax position in this period. He spent a lot of time in each of the UK and the US, and of course on ships making the journeys in between. He already had many sources of income, for apart from the 14 books which had been published by 1910, he was writing lyrics and his serials, short stories and articles were appearing in numerous journals. In *P G Wodehouse — Man and Myth*[1] Barry Phelps reports that he earned some £ 215 in 1903, his first full year as a professional writer, and £ 527 in 1907. Since liability to pay UK tax in 1907 started at an income level of no more than £ 130, it can be assumed that he was aware of the burden of taxation.

As far as complying with the rules of tax administration in the United States was concerned, it seems that he relied on his agents to prepare the necessary documentation. Afficionados will be aware of his unfortunate experience with the first of his agents, a certain Mr A E Baerman, who arranged for the publication of **Love Among The Chickens**[2] in the US under his own copyright, and demanded $ 250 from Wodehouse before he would relinquish his claim on it.

He then turned to R T B (Bobbie) Denby, who at least to start with was more reliable and who, according to the transcript of one of the US tax cases, filed tax returns on Wodehouse's behalf — and paid taxes calculated to be due. Questions did arise, noticeably about Wodehouse's status in the US (see the Appendix for a general discussion on this point), and whether sales of rights to his work, and royalties derived from his work, produced non-taxable income. The technical details of these points and arguments are not in the public domain, as a settlement was reached in 1923, without the matter coming before the Courts.

Towards the end of the period under consideration, the effect of the war, and the consequent need for governments to raise greater sums by way of taxation, were starting to make themselves felt, and the impact on the landed classes would be referred to time and time again by Wodehouse in his stories. Charles Graves illustrated the problem well in *The Bad Old Days*[3], when he referred to an article which he had written in about 1919 about the growing tendency of landowners to dine out. He quoted Mr R C Vaughan, the owner of fourteen hotels and restaurants:

> First class chefs are practically unobtainable by owners of private houses. Consequently the food is better and more daintily served in hotels. Taxation has prevented many landed proprietors from taking private houses for the London season. These people now live in hotels and give parties there...

No wonder Aunt Dahlia and Uncle Tom were prepared to do whatever was necessary to retain the services of Anatole!

During this period, tax does not have appeared to have been in any sense an obsession with Wodehouse personally. Even so, it started to have an important influence on his lifestyle. Around 1920, for instance, he seems to have realised that a substantial increase in his tax burden could arise if he spent a full tax year in the UK. On 21 February, 1921[4], he wrote in the following terms to Bill Townend:

> I'm off tomorrow to Paris on route for Biarritz. I find if I stay longer than six months in [England] I am liable to pay income tax on everything I make in America as well as in England, in addition to paying American income tax! This is no good to Pelham so I am skipping and should be away for about six weeks.

The six week period to which he refers was evidently designed to keep him out of the country until April 5, the end of the UK tax year.

Most of the Wodehouse writings during this period do not make undue reference to tax, although there are extensive references in two pieces of work and the first reference so far traced is to be found in 1902[5], when Wodehouse was just twenty.

> I always enjoy that scene in "Eric" where they pin the crib to Mr Gordon's desk. It is a luminous idea, and, if I remember rightly, worked admirably until it was discovered owing to the shocking bungling of Eric himself. "The Crib in Fiction" would not make much of an article, however. I can remember no other instance of actual cribbing in Form in the whole range of school literature (that is to say as much of the whole range of school literature as I have read). Cribbing out of school is, of course, common. Like a false income-tax return, it is expected of you.

His view of false income tax returns must have been obtained from discussions and hearsay — he was far too young and inexperienced to be able to benefit significantly himself. (Indeed, with a maximum tax rate of 1s 3d (6.25%), the profit to be earned from a false tax return was minuscule.) Almost the only occasion offering tacit approval to what would amount to tax evasion!

More studied are the references in the two longer works. First, the series of **Parrot** poems written for the *Daily Express* in September to December, 1903 (first drawn to our attention by Frances Donaldson[6], with extracts later included in a collection of poems entitled **The Parrot and Other Poems**[7]). This had a political theme (the price of food) and represented his contribution to the debate on the question of imperial preference and free trade. This inevitably carried a substantial number of explicit references to fiscal matters, as will be seen from the following extracts:

30 September, 1903

> When the Cobden Club relaxes into grief at "stomach taxes"
> A parrot perches daily just above the entrance door
> He doesn't mind what's said to him, or sung to him, or read to him
> For he can answer nothing but "YOUR FOOD WILL COST YOU MORE"

2 October, 1903

And this parrot daily mailing does not check its daily wailing;
Rather, squawks a little louder than it ever did before.
While its hearers vote, it waxes petulant on stomach taxes:
"Vote for Joe", and it is certain that — "YOUR FOOD WILL COST YOU MORE".

6 October, 1903

Now the parrot, bent on stopping
His depression, went a-hopping
Where a play by Mr Barrie
Sets the people in a roar.
Where with grins each face relaxes
There, he thought, that Stomach Taxes
He'd forget, and disremember
That "YOUR FOOD WILL COST YOU MORE".

21 October, 1903

"Can't you face this joyous cheering,"
So I cried, "and are you fearing
That the "stomach tax" is falsehood
And the Cobden Club a bore?
Do you hear in this a token
That your cause is burst and broken,
That the nation will not listen
To your "FOOD WILL COST YOU MORE"?"

12 November, 1903

Yet, doubt not on occasion,
When the "stomach tax" evasion
Forms the text for Hugh or Winnie,
Or the Public Orator,
That the Parrot, proudly stalking
From seclusion, will be talking
In his false and foolish manner,
"FOOD, DEAR FRIENDS, WILL COST YOU MORE."

This series of verses, produced daily for several weeks, represents what was probably the most politically orientated writing at any time in Wodehouse's long career. Anonymously presented in the paper, it nevertheless generated considerable interest at the time, and led to a "Parrot Screeching" contest which enabled Wodehouse's paymaster to generate significant unexpected publicity from the series. And the attribution to duties on food of the term "stomach taxes" shows a glimpse of the deft phrase that was to become his trademark.

The second extensive group of references to tax were contained in his version of **William Tell Told Again**[8], written in 1904, a tale of the consequences of objections raised by the Swiss people to the taxes being levied by the governor. In the extracts which follow, the taxes mentioned include several — eg those on sheep, cows, buns and lemonade — which do not recur in the remainder of his writings!

pp1,2   Gessler was not a nice man, and it soon became plain that he would never make himself really popular with the Swiss. The point on which they disagreed in particular was the question of taxes. The Swiss, who were a simple and thrifty people, objected to paying taxes of any sort. They said they wanted to spend their money on all kinds of other things. Gessler, on the other hand, wished to put a tax on everything, and, being Governor, he did it. He made everyone who owned a flock of sheep pay a certain sum of money to him; and if the farmer sold his sheep and bought cows, he had to pay rather more money to Gessler for the cows than he had paid for the sheep. Gessler also taxed bread, and biscuits, and jam, and buns, and lemonade, and, in fact, everything he could think of, till the people of Switzerland determined to complain.

p4   "The fact is, your Excellency, it seems to the people of Switzerland ... "

" ... Whom I represent," whispered Arnold of Melchthal.

" ... Whom I represent, that things want changing."

"What things?" enquired Gessler.

"The taxes, your excellent Governorship."

"Change the taxes? Why, don't the people of Switzerland think there are enough taxes?"

Arnold of Melchthal broke in hastily.

"They think there are many too many," he said. "What with the tax on sheep, and the tax on cows, and the tax on bread, and the tax on tea, and the tax ... "

"I know, *I* know," Gessler interrupted; "I know all the taxes. Come to the point. What about 'em?"

"Well, your Excellency, there are too many of them."

pp5,6 "This gentleman here" — [Gessler] pointed to Arnold of Melchthal — "says he does not like taxes, and that he isn't going to put up with them any longer."

pp7,8 [After having arranged for the tip of Arnold's finger to be dipped in boiling oil]

33

... Gessler leaned forward again.

"Have your views on taxes changed at all?" he asked. "Do you see my point of view more clearly now?"

Arnold admitted that he thought that, after all, there might be something to be said for it.

"That's right," said the Governor. "And the tax on sheep? You don't object to that?"

"No."

"And the tax on cows?"

"I like it"

"And those on bread, and buns, and lemonade?"

"I enjoy them."

pp10,11 "Has he taken off the tax on jam?" asked Ulric the smith.

"What is he going to do about the tax on mixed biscuits?" shouted Klaus von der Flue, who was a chimney-sweep of the town and loved mixed biscuits.

p12 "In short," continued Walter, "after a few minutes' very interesting conversation he made us see that it really wouldn't do, and that we must go on paying taxes as before."

34

p14   [Another Arnold felt let down, and that he could have done better]

" ... I should have said that I hoped his Excellency had enjoyed a good dinner. Once on the subject of food, and it would have been the simplest of tasks to show him how unnecessary taxes on food were, and the whole affair would have been pleasantly settled while you waited ... "

p15   "Then he really won't let us off the taxes?" asked the crowd in disappointed voices.

"No"

"Then the long and the short of it is," said Walter Furst, drawing a deep breath, "that we must rebel!"

p16   "Down with the tyrant!" shouted Walter Furst.

"Down with the taxes!" shrieked the crowd.

p19   "Aha!" said Tell. "Oho! so it's you, is it? *I* know you. And a nice sort of person you are, with your taxes on bread and sheep, aren't you! ... "

p22   In fact, Tell and his family lived a very happy, contented life, in spite of the Governor Gessler and his taxes.

The remainder of the book concentrates on the attempt by the Swiss to rebel, and gain their freedom from Gessler, the Emperor and in consequence from taxes. One might say that it contained some ideas ahead of its time in using the concept of assassination to solve the problem of excessive taxes, but that concept was to recur in the lyric which was written for *Sitting Pretty* in 1924, from which this book has taken its title.

Another rich source of his comments about taxes and tax-collectors is *Punch*, although not particularly so during this early period, during which there are only four items. First, in the poem *The Lost Leader*, concerning the retirement of the Rev Sir Owen Kettle, K.C.B., in the 4 March, 1903 issue:

> You were not built for the joys of peace, your business
>   is on the sea
> The bridge of a tramp is the place for you, my reverend
>   K.C.B.
> You were not born to be slothful, sleek, a payer of tax
>   and rate
> Leave such a life to lesser men — yours is a nobler fate.

Rather more tongue-in-cheek was the article *Balm For The Broken-Hearted*, on 24 February, 1904. Part of this consisted of a letter from "Energetic Journalist" to an editor:

> My Very Dear Sir
>
> Take my advice, and look on the bright side. What seems a misfortune at first sight, often proves in the end to be a blessing. Many years ago I was engaged for six months to a lady who afterwards refused to marry me. What was the result? Misery? Gloom? Not a bit of it. I wrote and placed to great advantage articles on "How to Propose", "Buying the Ring", "Do Girls like Presents?", "The £ s.d. of Courtship", "Should Kisses be Taxed?" and "How to Write a Love-Letter"...... "

In an article **The First Paying Guest**, 14 June, 1905, one of the two characters involved is Ion Smithios, a Greek Ratepayer living in the year 1004 BC. Finally, in this period, in the collection of Charivaria on 2 April, 1913, he drew attention to two young men, charged with disorderly conduct in the street, who pleaded that they were ratepayers and had a right to sing and dance. "Ratepayers", in an English context at least, means someone paying local property taxes, and references are properly included in this summary!

Wodehouse's first entry into the theatrical world also came in 1904, when he was invited to write additional lyrics for **Sergeant Brue**, at the *Strand* theatre. Although he was not responsible for the text of the book, it is interesting to note the following exchange:

Daisy   Here's a letter for you, Sergeant

Brue   A letter!

Michael   Who's it from?

Daisy   I don't know — a messenger boy brought it.

Aurora   What's it about?

Daisy   I haven't been able to read it yet — you've got the kettle up here.

(Exit Daisy)

Brue   A letter for me. It can't be the King's taxes, they don't come by messenger boy, they're in too much of a hurry.

In 1908, he made references to taxes being due in a spoof Book of Days included in **The Globe By The Way Book**[9]:

Our Rapid Calendar — December 1908	Weather Forecast
....	
25 Christmas Day!!! Rent, rates, and taxes due	Rain
....	
27 Rent, rates and taxes still due.	Raining
....	
31 Christmas bills, rent, rates and taxes still unpaid	Raining

And in another extract from the book, one can find a reference to yet another unusual tax :

Who's Who (Our Lightning Edition)

Balfour, Rt. Hon. Arthur James, P.C., F.R.S., D.L., East Lothian; philosophic doubter; M.P. (C.), City of London since 1906; *b.* July 25, 1848. Had good situation, 1902-1906, but in last-named year went to the country for a change, and, on returning, found his place had been filled; became a Preferential Free-Trader, 1903; adopted the cause of Tariff Reform, 1904. *Publications:* Economic notes on the Taxation of Schenectady Putters, 1903; ....

The Oldest Member does not seem to have made use of this particular implement, and neither does it feature in the bags of clubs which his friends and acquaintances, or their caddies, carry round the course.

Shortly before the first world war, Wodehouse undertook some work in co-operation with Charles Bovill. One piece was a theatrical revue, **Nuts & Wine**, at the Empire theatre, and this featured a song, called *The Chancellor of the Exchequer*, which mentioned a wide range of taxes and was sung by a bus conductor as the theatrical bus travelled through London:

I'm not a Member. No, not I
Of your belted Aristocracy
In the Strand, Piccadilly, Rotten Row or the Cut.
If Taffy's Budget then I should reach
Then I am stranded on the beach
In the Strand, on your uppers — Stony broke — Busted.
Then we'll all go Tango teasing
We will, by George!
Of a Tax on land why make a fuss?
It still remains but a penny on a bus
In the Strand for the sake of the Chancellor of the Exchequer.

To pay the extra taxes, I
Must take my Moet extra Dry
In the Strand, Lockharts — Romano's — outside
If there's another bit on the income stuck
My income I intend to chuck.
In the Strand — Waterloo! Water-loss! What ho!
And racing men will suffer — they will poor things
For racing comes as a matter of course
There's a bit upon the backer
Put a bit upon the horse
In the Strand for the sake of the Chancellor of the Exchequer.

Lloyd wrote his scheme, and he will not smudge it
And he won't budge an inch
Not an inch from his Budget.
When it comes
We must pay
Or be presented at the Court.

Through a cycle tax our hearts would harrow
I'd stick to the wheel for I'd share along a barrow
In the Strand — no change — On change — Change here.
Oh, take the tax off glucose.
Oh do! Please do.
Be kind to the thirsty, beery man
It's a tanner on the barrel and a penny on the can
In the Strand for the sake of the Chancellor of the Exchequer.

Why don't they tax all pastry cooked
For on pastry I have never looked
In the Strand, Regent Street — Pass along, Mind the step
Tax for the good of the Revenue
The crusty bits and the crummy bits too
In the Strand, Eccles Cakes — Turnovers — Maids of Honour.
Yes put a tax on pastry — if not, why not
The contents of each pastry cart
A penny on a pancake and twopence on a tart
In the Strand for the sake of the Chancellor of the Exchequer.

Why not tax all domestic pets
Alligators and Suffragettes
In the Strand, Trafalgar Square, Hyde Park and on the Links
Tax bachelors and married men
Whether for good, or only now and then
Houseboats, hotels, flats, Abodes of Love -
These attacks on a tax on taxis
Flags up
So are the roads
There's a Tax on Stocks and Shares should be
But let Marconigrams go free, do you see
For the sake of the Chancellor of the Exchequer.

There were two other references in the show to taxes of one sort
or another. In the opening dialogue of Act II, Mr Punch is talking
to a representative of His Majesty's police force:

Police   ... On your right you will observe the Gerrard
Street Telephone Exchange.

Punch   But why has that been moved here?

Police	Well, you see, sir, when the County Council found they'd no use for the Aldwych Island site they turned it into a sort of refuge where public nuisances are deported. It's now Ellis Island Aldwych site. What we've got here is an asylum containing public buildings and folk that are driving other people insane. (points) There's Somerset House, the home of the Income Tax nuisance.

An early indication of the feelings which were to rise in strength over the next sixty years!

And in a song added later during the run, which in singing style is a parody of *When a Felon's not Engaged in his Employment* from **Pirates of Penzance**, we find:

When a statesman starts talking through his chapeau
— Through his chapeau

And he puts a tax upon uncultured land
— Cultured land

No matter if that land is off the map — O
— Off the map — O

It is nice to see his countenance expand
— Ance expand

The next year, 1914, Wodehouse and Bovill retained as their target taxes on land, making the following point in the story **The Episode of The Hired Past**[10]:

[Lord Evenwood is lecturing his daughter, Eva, on the reasons why Roland Bleke would represent a better marriage than her cousin Gerry O'Rion.]

41

"Young O'Rion is not to be thought of," said Lord Evenwood firmly. "Not for an instant. Apart from anything else, his politics are all wrong. Moreover, you are engaged to this Mr. Bleke. It is a sacred responsibility not lightly to be evaded. You cannot pledge your word one day to enter upon the most solemn contract known to — ah — the civilized world, and break it the next. It is not fair to the man. It is not fair to me. You know that all I live for is to see you comfortably settled. If I could myself do anything for you, the matter would be different. But these abominable land taxes and Blowick — especially Blowick — no, no, it's out of the question. You will be very sorry if you do anything foolish. I can assure you that Roland Blekes are not to be found — ah — on every bush. Men are very shy of marrying nowadays."

During this period, Wodehouse was very prolific in the work he was producing for *Vanity Fair*. He had a number of roles, including theatre critic, essay writer and fiction writer, and on a number of occasions wrote essays or articles about some aspect of the theatre. In the following extracts from the American edition he manages to bring taxation to the fore as a cause of the intermittent slump in audience numbers:

THE POOR OLD DRAMA — Vanity Fair, 1/18

For the Theatre has got it right on the back collar-stud. What with the war-tax and the income-tax and the super-tax and Red Cross Benefits and Liberty Loans and women who knit instead of attending matinees, the Drama is experiencing the worst slump in many years, and the writings of a dramatic critic on a monthly magazine are coming to have a merely archaeological interest.

THE THEATRICAL SLUMP — Vanity Fair, 2/18

[A purported interview between PGW and impresario Charles B Dillingham.]

"What, in your opinion, Mr Dillingham," I enquired, "is the chief cause of the badness of theatrical business at the moment of going to press?"

"In my opinion, there are five reasons for the present slump in theatrical prosperity this year. First, too many theatres. Second, cut-rate ticket-agencies. Third, excessive tax. Fourth, inferiority of material owing to over-production. Fifth, the shock of the first realization on the part of the public of how much depends on us in the war."

But he adds, very fairly, that an even greater cause is the lack of suitable material.

THE TRIALS OF A HARD WINTER — Vanity Fair, 2/18

It is my opinion that what is wrong with the present theatrical season is not the War or the Tax or the Weather or the Movies or the fact that Sister Susie is knitting socks for soldiers instead of rolling up to the Wednesday matinee, but the poor quality of the plays presented.

THE BARRYMORES, AND OTHERS — Vanity Fair, 4/18

It behooves these high-foreheaded, long-haired geniuses who float dreamily above the world in a world of their own, to realize that we earthly devils, when we pay out two crackling bucks, plus the *unavailable* war-tax, demand two-and-a-half hours' entertainment.

It is reasonable to suppose that the italicised word "unavailable" was printed as an interesting but unintentional variation on "inevitable"!

REVIEWING A THEATRE AUDIENCE — Vanity Fair, 11/19

... that is why it is wrong to say unkind things about the audience. The man who goes to see a play is a sportsman, and should be entitled to consideration as such.

What it amounts to is that he has betted — blindly — good money and war-tax that he will not be bored. If he loses his bet, it is very decent of him merely to sit still and say nothing.

THE NEW PLAYS — Vanity Fair, 5/20

Once upon a time there was a theatrical manager who decided to take no chances. "Hitherto," he said to his partner, "I have been putting plays on blindly and trusting to luck. From now on I am going to work the thing on a system. I intend to employ the services of a professional psychologist, one of those fellows who have their finger on the public pulse and watch tendencies and see which way the wind is blowing and all that sort of thing."

"Good enough," said the partner, who left all the executive side of the business to the other, concentrating his own energies on slipping jokers in authors' contracts and seeing that they got less than their rightful share of the movie money. "Go to it."

So the manager wrote to the correspondence school and told them to send along their best man. And presently the psychologist arrived.

"Now," said the psychologist, "touching this matter of what the public wants. The public today, let us remember, is composed of people who have just been suffering the strain of a war. They have had to pay out all their savings in income tax. Living is expensive. There has been an awful lot of snow, and in all probability they have come out without their rubbers. What do they want? Distraction. Give them light, pleasant, gentle, mild plays, and watch 'em bite!"

"Fine!" cried the manager enthusiastically. "I'll do it!"

"On the other hand," went on the psychologist, "we must always remember that the public of today is composed of people who have just been suffering the strain of a war. They have had to pay out all their savings in income tax. Living is expensive. There has been an awful lot of snow, and in all probability they have come out without their rubbers. What do they want? Distraction. They want to go to the theatre and see people worse off than themselves. Give them, therefore, strong, tense, gloomy, tragic plays where the fellow comes home with his feet wet after paying his income-tax and finds that his wife loves another, the maid has given notice, and the cat has been at the cold chicken."

"Then you mean," said the manager, "that it's just the same old gamble? There's nothing you can do except take a chance?"

"Precisely," said the psychologist. "By the way, could I have my first month's salary in advance?"

The other piece he wrote for **Vanity Fair** which had a tax relevance was **All About The Income Tax**[11], a delightful piece showing that the task of completing the annual return was akin to a parlour game in which the whole family could join. It was later expanded into a full-length essay for **Louder and Funnier**[12], a book of derivative essays published in the UK but not the US, and can be found on pages 52 to 55.

One reference to tax which related to this period and was not unduly disparaging did not appear in print until the publication of **Bring On The Girls**[13] in 1954, but relates to the period after completing **A Damsel in Distress** and the musical **Oh, My Dear!** and while working on **Indiscretions of Archie:**

> They went into the gambling rooms, which were filled with men in dress-clothes and women laden down with jewels. Europe had not yet regained its pre-war popularity, and everybody was coming to Palm Beach. The recently established tax on income, crushing though it was — four per cent, if we remember rightly — had not removed any of the gilt from the gilded set. The two writers, who had but recently acquired the feeling of solvency, shrank back into the ranks of the under-privileged as they saw the walnut-sized diamonds and the piles of green twenty-dollar chips strewn across the roulette wheel.

In **Indiscretions of Archie**[14] itself, he makes a reference to war-tax which suggests that tax is starting to be a topic which is at the forefront of Wodehouse's mind, and is likely to stay there. It adds something to his prose, but....

> [Archie has been handed a basket containing the snake belonging to Mme Brudowska, a star whose expression of horror and fury, combined with a deep voice and sinuous walk, enabled her to draw down a matter of a thousand dollars a week. The voice has produced a piercing scream; the expression had gone through Archie like a knife.]

Indeed, though the fact gave him little pleasure, Archie, as a matter of fact, was at this moment getting about — including war-tax — two dollars and seventy-five cents worth of the great emotional star for nothing.

The following year Wodehouse wrote **The Adventures of Sally**[15], and showed in the following brief extract that there had been no inflation in the price of theatre seats over the previous twelve months.

"You go," said [Sally's dancing partner] earnestly. "You *go!*" Take it from me, it's a swell show. You seen *Myrtle takes a Turkish Bath*?"

"I don't go to many theatres."

"You go! It's a scream. I been to a show every night since I got here. Every night regular. Swell shows all of 'em, except this last one. I cert'nly picked a lemon to-night all right. I was taking a chance, y'see, because it was an opening. Thought it would be something to say, when I got back home, that I'd been to a New York opening. Set me back two-seventy-five, including tax, and I wish I'd got it in my kick right now..."

The final group of references in this period all appear in the books or lyrics of musical comedies of which he was joint author. The first time it seems to have been included in a lyric, as far as the writer has been able to trace, was in *Oh, Boy!*, in 1917, in which, incidentally, the names of some of the characters seem to have been chosen by eleven-year-old schoolchildren (Lotta Noyes. Annie Olde-Knight. Ivan L. Ovanerve. Phelan Fyne. And Rhoda Byke.) The second stanza of the song *Flubby-Dub* reads as follows:

Flubby-dub the Caveman lived the ideal life
Far from all this modern noise and care and strife
He got up each morning with the sun
Took the dinosawrus for a run

47

When the rent collector called on quarter day
He got out his club and when men called for taxes
He'd just sharpen up his axes
Life was pretty soft for Flubby-dub.

The second inclusion in a musical was in the song *Wheatless Days*, from **Oh, Lady! Lady!!**, which started its pre-New York tour in late 1917, and was the seventh Wodehouse show of that year.

We'll be so happy at our cozy little flat;
When ends the honeymoon:
I'll think up dodges to avoid the income tax,
While you prepare the evening prune.
And when our simple meal is done,
To keep from getting bored,
We'll talk about the sugar,
Which once we could afford.
Perhaps a little stranger
Will come to us one day:
But if the janitor objects,
We'll give the child away.

The third reference was in **Kissing Time**, during a threeway conversation between Col Bollinger, Bi-Bi St Pol (husband of the actress Georgette) and Lucienne Touquet:

[Bi-Bi St Pol is carrying a trunk on his shoulders.]

Col Bol   How dare you insult this little woman.

Bi-Bi   You think she's a little woman? You ought to get a peek at the midget that sunk me! She was the littlest woman I ever saw.

[The Colonel turns away up RC in disgust.]

Col Bol   Say what have you got in this trunk?

Lucienne Is it heavy?

Bi-Bi   Heavy? I think it's got George Robey's income tax in it.

In *The Golden Moth*, written with Fred Thompson and completed in October 1921, there are three separate examples. The first occurs when Dipper Tigg (alias the Marquis) is speaking to Rose, a lady's maid impersonating Aline de Crillon, the lady in question, about the property which they have just reached:

Marquis   Why, it's a villa — how are you rated here?

Rose   Rated?

Marquis   Yes, don't you know what rates are?

Rose   No — I've never heard of them.

Marquis   What?

American readers may appreciate a reminder that until 1990, rates were the UK equivalent of property taxes, the amount charged varying partly by reference to the value of the premises. It is hard to see why this should have been relevant to Rose or to the development of the play, as the action was set in France!

Despite the fact that taxation levels were not particularly high, income taxes were clearly resented by the general public (well, at least the theatre-going public, who were more likely than most to be paying income tax) at this time, as can be seen from the second reference, this time from Act 2:

Marquis   But look here, if its aristocratic crooks you want, why worry to look further?

Rose   What do you mean?

Marquis   Well, if the Blackbird's the King of them, I'm the Ace.

Rose   Do you really mean to tell me that you're a robber?

Marquis   A <u>robber</u>? Well, I nearly became an Income
         Tax Assessor.

And in Act 3, the joy of a tax-free society is expressed in the
second stanza of *The Island of Never Mind Where*:

> It's a Paradise, where no sorrow or sin come
> Income Tax is nothing, for they haven't any income!
> No one pays milliners' bills,
> Girls don't put on any frills!
> In the Island of Never-mind-where-
> Never-mind-where.

In **The Cabaret Girl**, (written with George Grossmith in September
1922), there was also a song which lamented the inevitability of
tax payments:

> When all your bills and your taxes are due
> And to the workhouse you're feeling that you
> May go, may go!
>
> When you are caught in the rain with no um-
> Brella and think you are sure to get lum-
> -Bago, -bago!
>
> Buck up and yodel "Whoop-de-OOdle-do!"
> That's the only thing that's left to do.

Finally, in **The Beauty Prize**, also written jointly with George
Grossmith, this time in August 1923, there was a manuscript
alteration to the submitted second verse of *It's a Long, Long, Day*,
almost certainly in PG's hand, on the only available copy of the
book script.

The alteration was to insert the line in italics below, and tack the
underlined words on to the line on which it now appears, instead
of having a line to itself:

I know sometimes I'd like to adopt
Old Rip Van Winkle's tip
And go to sleep for twenty odd years
And thus avoid all fuss
Just follow his plan and safe in your bed <u>you'll be</u>
When tax-collectors call round with their Schedule B
No doubt about it, he knew the way
To pass the long, long day.

This verse does not appear in the printed score, so it may have been edited out after rehearsal, but it again illustrates the Wodehouse antipathy to taxation.

Footnotes

1   1992, Constable
2   1906, Circle Publishing Co
3   1951, Faber and Faber
4   Performing Flea. 1953, Herbert Jenkins
5   January 1902, Public School Magazine
6   P G Wodehouse. 1982, Weidenfeld and Nicholson
7   1988, Hutchinson
8   1904, A&C Black
9   1908, Globe Publishing Co
10 September 1914, Strand. Included in *A Man of Means*. 1991, Porpoise Books
11 May 1919, Vanity Fair
12 1932, Faber and Faber
13 1954, Herbert Jenkins
14 1921, Herbert Jenkins
15 1922, Herbert Jenkins

All About the Income-Tax
A New Parlor Game for the Family Circle

AS I sit in my poverty-stricken home, looking at the place where the piano used to be before I had to sell it to pay my income-tax, I find myself in thoughtful mood. The first agony of the separation from my hard-earned, so to speak, income, is over, and I can see that I was unjust in my original opinion of the United States Government. At first, I felt towards the U. S. G. as I would feel toward any perfect stranger who insinuated himself into my home and stood me on my head and went through my pockets. The only difference I could see between the U. S. G. and the ordinary practitioner in a black mask was that the latter occasionally left his victim carfare.

Gosh! I was bitter.

NOW, however, after the lapse of weeks, I begin to see the other side. What the Government is going to do with it, I do not know — I can only hope that they will not spend it on foolishness and nut sundaes and the movies — but, apparently, they needed a few billion dollars, and you and I had to pay it. That part remains as unpleasant as ever. But what I, like so many others, have overlooked is the thoughtfulness of the authorities in having chosen March for the final filling-up of their printed forms.

The New Indoor Sport

YOU know how it is in the long Winter evenings, if you have nothing to occupy you. You either play auction bridge, or you go in for one of those games played with colored counters and a painted board (than which nothing is more sapping to the soul), or else you sit and scowl at each other and send the children early to bed. But, last March, with the arrival of Form 10536 X-G, dullness in the home became impossible. Our paternal government, always on the lookout for some way of brightening the lives of the Common People, had invented the greatest round-game in the world. Tiddley-winks has been completely superseded.

In every home, during the past Winter, it was possible to see the delightful spectacle of a united family concentrated on the new game. There was Father with his spectacles on, with Mother leaning over his shoulder and pointing out that, by taking Sec. 6428 H and shoving it on top of Sub-Sec 9730, he could claim immunity from the tax mentioned in Sec 4587 M. Clustered around the table were the children, sucking pencils and working out ways of beating the surtax.

"See, papa," cries little Cyril, "what I have found! You are exempt from paying tax on income derived from any public utility or the exercise of any essential government function accruing to any state or territory or any political sub-division thereof or to the District of Columbia, or income accruing to the United States or any political sub-division thereof. That means you can knock off the price of the canary's birdseed!"

"And, papa," chimes in little Wilbur, "I note that Gifts (not made as a consideration for service rendered) and money and property acquired under a will or inheritance (but the income derived from money or property received by gift, will, or inheritance) are taxable and must be reported. Therefore, by referring to Sub-Sec. 2864905, we find that you can skin the blighters for the price of the openwork socks we gave the janitor at Christmas."

And so the game went on, each helping the other, all working in that perfect harmony which one so seldom sees in families nowadays.

53

NOR is this all. Think how differently the head of the family regards his nearest and dearest in these days of income-tax. Many a man who has spent years wondering why he was such a chump as to link his lot with a woman he has disliked from the moment they stepped out of the Niagara Falls Hotel, and a gang of children whose existence has always seemed superfluous, gratefully revises his views as he starts to fill up the printed form.

His wife may be a nuisance about the home, but she comes out strong when it is a question of the married man's exemption. And the children! As the father looks at their grubby faces, and reflects that he is entitled to knock off two hundred bones per child, the austerity of his demeanor softens, and he pats them on the head and talks vaguely about jam for tea at some future and unspecified date.

There is no doubt that the income-tax, whatever else it has done, has taught the family to value one another. It is the first practical step that has been taken against the evil of race-suicide.

One beauty of this income-tax game is that it is educational. It enlarges the vocabulary and teaches one to think. Take, for instance, the clause on Amortization.

In pre-income-tax days, if anyone had talked to me of amortization, I should, no doubt, have kept up my end of the conversation adroitly and given a reasonable display of intelligence, but all the while I should have been wondering whether amortization was a new religion or a form of disease which attacks parrots.

Now, however, I know all about it. You should have seen me gaily knocking off whatever I thought wouldn't be missed for amortization of the kitchen sink.

You would hardly believe it — though I trust the income-tax authorities will — what an awful lot of amortization there was at my little place last year. The cat got amortized four times, once by a spark from the fire, the other three times by stray dogs: and it got so bad with the goldfish that they became practically permanent amorters.

Heaven Help the Corporations!

AS REGARDS income-tax, I am, thank goodness, an individual. I pray that I never become a corporation. It seems to me that some society for the prevention of cruelty to things ought to step in between the authorities and the corporations. I have never gone very deeply into the matter, having enough troubles of my own, but a casual survey of the laws relating to the taxing of corporations convinces me that any corporation that gets away with its trousers and one collar-stud should offer up Hosannahs.

The general feeling about the income-tax appears to have been that it is all right this time, but it mustn't happen again. I was looking through a volume of *Punch*, for 1882, the other day, and I came across a gloomy-looking individual paying his tax.

"I can just do it this time," he is saying, "but I wish you would tell Her Majesty that she mustn't look on me as a source of income in the future."

No indoor game ever achieves popularity for two successive years, and the Government must think up something new for next Winter.

CHAPTER 4: 1924 to 1931 — THE STORMCLOUDS GATHER

This was the period during which the storm clouds really started to gather, but the problems that Wodehouse was to have in relation to his tax affairs had not yet been drawn to the attention of the tax authorities. He demonstrated questionable judgment in relation to his choice of professional financial advisers, particularly John W Rumsey, and later Bobbie Denby, but balanced that to some degree by strengthening his relationship with the most loyal of all his representatives, Paul Reynolds, his US literary agent. As will be observed over the next few chapters, Reynolds was continually trying to ensure that he understood his responsibilities and the extent to which his freedom of action in monetary affairs had to be constrained.

Much of the available information about this period is derived from the correspondence between Wodehouse and Paul Reynolds, which can be found at Columbia University. Much preliminary work on these letters was undertaken by Prof Evelyne d'Auzac, whose detailed analysis facilitated the author's own researches into that correspondence.

The first serious tax problem which Wodehouse faced arose quite simply from the utter incompetence of one John W Rumsey, his US agent for musical contracts and a "playbroker" working for the American Play Company. Rumsey suggested that a company be formed "to take care of the taxes of Mr Wodehouse", an expression that we can charitably assume to be a euphemism for "to help reduce the taxes of Mr Wodehouse". Because of Wodehouse's status as a Non-Resident Alien for US tax purposes, he was only liable to a withholding tax of 5-6% on his US source earnings, and nothing on foreign earnings.

One can only speculate as to Rumsey's motives, but he surely would not have suggested forming a US company without having in mind some other actions, such as eliminating its income by paying out as deductible expenses such items as salaries and travel costs. There would have been no sense in planning for the company to retain all its earnings, because a US corporation would pay high federal and state taxes on its entire profits. One can make an educated guess that Rumsey neither explained his thinking to anyone else nor made sure the administrative niceties of his plans were followed up.

In the event, despite the strongly felt view expressed in *All About the Income Tax* (see page 55) that Wodehouse should never become a corporation, the idea was adopted, Jeeves Dramatics, Inc. being formed. It opened its first bank account at the Guaranty Trust Company on 5 January, 1927, and had its commercial office at 33 West 42nd Street.

So far, so good.

One of the most difficult problems which professional tax advisers come across in the business world is that of convincing clients that even where there are good and valid reasons for such steps as the formation of a company, such steps carry with them commensurate responsibilities, and certain formal obligations must be carried out if the plan is to be effective. Those obligations include holding company meetings, maintaining records of corporate decisions, keeping proper accounts and properly separating cash flows belonging to the corporation from those of its owners.

These responsibilities were largely ignored or overlooked by Rumsey, and although in an ideal world one might have expected Wodehouse and Reynolds to monitor this, it would not have been the norm in the 1920s for the busy proprietor of a company to have taken a close personal interest in the corporate administration. For make no mistake, Wodehouse was a busy man — in the 1920s alone he wrote 10 novels and around a hundred short stories, apart from his involvement as playwright, author or lyricist of 18 theatrical productions, many of which appeared on both sides of the Atlantic.

Wodehouse and Reynolds were kept in blissful ignorance of any problems until some time in 1929, shortly after the termination of Rumsey's involvement with the company by Wodehouse at the end of the previous year. Coincidentally, PG and Ethel transferred their personal banking affairs to National City Bank, and Guaranty Trust Co (the ongoing bankers to Jeeves Dramatics), who had accepted instructions to make cash transfers between personal and company accounts without worrying about the formalities, now decided to act somewhat more responsibly. They declined to make certain cash transfers and advances which the Wodehouses had requested, on the grounds that Jeeves Dramatics Inc had not authorised them. Only then did Reynolds and Wodehouse find that not only had no formalities been arranged for the company by Rumsey, but neither had any tax returns been filed.

In a letter of 23 October, 1929, Reynolds wrote to Wodehouse:

> I understand there is a question of the corporation's relations which ultimately must be settled. If Rumsey is no longer to be a director of the corporation, and you want me to be responsible, I should first like to take all the papers to my lawyers who are first class and whose charges are reasonable. I think that they would bring the affairs up to date and settle any tax question that may arise and everything would be in order.

Wodehouse accepted this advice in a letter of 4 November, 1929:

> I think the best plan about Jeeves Inc. is to do as you suggest and have your son succeed Rumsey as treasurer ... As regards the income tax, I think you'd better see your lawyer, as you suggest, and find out what ought to be done ... hire some accountant to tell us exactly what income tax Jeeves Inc. had to pay and then you tell me and we pay it.

Not the sort of response you would expect from someone deliberately trying to evade his responsibilities in relation to reporting and paying his taxes.

On 19 November Reynolds was writing again, to say that he had already taken the papers to his lawyer, Mr Malone, of Perkins, Malone and Washburn:

An American corporation is taxable ... by both our federal government and our State governments and the taxes are pretty high. As far as we can find out the corporation never filed any tax returns or paid any taxes, so there is a danger that back taxes will be due, and also penalties for failure to report or pay back taxes.

Of course this situation ultimately has got to be taken care of. If the American tax authorities did not discover the tax situation in the next few years, they could not help discover it on your death, and then your estate might be eaten up by back taxes and litigation.

.....

Our lawyers are inclined to the opinion that it would be wisest to dissolve the corporation and wind up its affairs and make other disposition of your income to bring the American taxes to the minimum. They of course have got to take into consideration your British income tax and be sure that in reducing your tax at this end they are not increasing it at the other end. They are not, however, prepared to advise that step until they have gone into the matter further and estimated what back taxes are due.

This was followed up in a matter of days with two cables and another letter, in which Reynolds made the bald statement:

As far as I can find out the entire matter of Jeeves Dramatics has been atrociously handled from the time of the formation of the corporation.

The accountants to Jeeves Dramatics, Acker, Bacas and McGirl, sent a report to Halsey Malone, who incorporated the information so produced into a detailed letter to Paul Reynolds on 3 December, 1929. Malone was the first person to look at the facts without having had prior involvement with Wodehouse or his affairs, and his view of the position can be regarded as reliable. The following extracts both confirm Reynolds' view of the company, and clarify certain basic facts:

> The corporation was formed in November 1926, and on November 8th of that year, the formal organization and the first meeting of directors was held, at which a proposition from Mr Wodehouse to assign certain contracts theretofore made by him and all other contracts to be made by him during the period of the next ten years for his literary work, in return for all of the capital stock of the corporation, was considered and accepted. This assignment is incomplete in certain respects and we are advised that it has been informally modified from time to time, although there is no record of these modifications.

> In fact, the records and data with which we have been furnished indicate that no corporate action of any kind has been taken since this first meeting of directors in 1926, although the corporation seems to have engaged in many transactions. Nor does it appear that the corporation has ever made any State franchise or Federal income tax returns for the years 1926, 1927 and 1928, or ever to have paid any taxes in connection therewith, which of course gives rise to rather a serious situation.

> .....

> ... we enclose for your information, approximation of the Federal income tax and State franchise taxes for those years, totalling $ 32,753.56. This figure includes interest from the due date of such taxes and the

maximum penalties, and it is calculated on the basis of actual receipts and disbursements ... without making any deductions for salaries and other items of expense which would be allowed as deductions when substantiated by proper proof.

The lawyers go on to suggest they be allowed to approach the tax authorities to seek "as favorable a compromise as may be possible". Their report was forwarded to Wodehouse by Paul Reynolds on 6 December, who endorsed the recommendation that they be allowed to contact the tax authorities, but added in an informal covering note:

> ... I am awfully sorry about all this tax business, but the only way seems to be to face it and have it done with. Troubles never seem to come singly in this world but I think even though it involves paying a large sum of money, when you have once got it out of the way you will breathe easier and know it isn't still to come. If there was any way that I could get you out of it, I hope you know that I would.

In a P.S. he added:

> Mr Rumsey states that he has never filed any statement of income on your account with the proper authorities, and never paid any amount on your account in taxes to the government.

When Rumsey's services were terminated by Wodehouse, Harold Ober, who worked for Reynolds, either became Treasurer or started going through the formalities which would have made him so. This step was not a particular success — in a file note written some time in 1930 by Paul Revere Reynolds to his father, he reminded him that when Rumsey got out,

Harold Ober and Denby took over the papers and started to elect Ober an officer, and then Ober and Denby dropped it, as far as you can find out because they were afraid that if they brought it to Wodehouse's attention, Wodehouse would be mad. Part of the reason why you and Ober split was due to the handling of Wodehouse's work.

He also pointed out that

Ober had undertaken to handle the matter "last spring" (ie 1929) and Denby also knew about it and neither of them did one thing in regard to it and after we parted with Ober [23 September, 1929] we took it up and got the best legal advice that we could.

When Harold Ober left Reynolds to set up business on his own account, Reynolds proposed that his son, Paul Revere Reynolds, should be appointed vice-president and treasurer, but that Reynolds senior should have power of attorney and would retain legal responsibilities -

I am to be responsible for any tax that may be due from such corporation.

A statement in such forthright terms, coupled with the other background to the creation and running of Jeeves Dramatics, Inc, may well be considered to go some way towards clearing Wodehouse from any accusation that he was culpable in respect of any irregularities, beyond the basic responsibility which rests on any controlling shareholder of a corporation. Even in recent years, such shareholders have traditionally considered their responsibilities to have been fulfilled if they appointed suitable professionals to administer the corporation, and Wodehouse certainly thought that Rumsey and Denby were suitable for this purpose.

One of the consequences of the investigations into the tax position of Jeeves Dramatics, coupled with the more formal stance now being taken by the bank, was that all parties advised that the Jeeves Dramatics Inc bank account would have to be blocked for a while, in order to avoid complicating the situation further, and also to ensure there would be sufficient funds to discharge whatever debts were found to be due to the tax authorities.

Despite the fact that Reynolds was the most professional of all his advisers, Wodehouse did not regard him as a financial adviser. He therefore decided to have Acker, Bacas and McGirl, accountants, transfer all the Jeeves Dramatics, Inc. files to Bobbie Denby, and Reynolds's responsibility for Jeeves Dramatics tax affairs seems to have come to an end on 17 February, 1930. The difficulties with Jeeves Dramatics, Inc's tax position had still not been brought to the attention of the Revenue authorities.

But Denby did not prove to be an ideal replacement, one reason being that he fell ill almost as soon as he was appointed, and had no involvement with the tax authorities for over a year, until Spring 1931. As early as April 1930 Ethel wrote to Reynolds to say she had heard nothing from Denby, and that she was anxious to fix up their income tax. And by the end of May, PG was writing from MGM in California extolling the virtues of the place, and commenting on the fact that his income tax is knocked off before he receives his pay every Saturday. (The tax rate applied to his earnings appears still to have been 5%.)

One might reasonably conclude that although Wodehouse made the right noises about being prepared to face up to his responsibilities, he would nevertheless have preferred to have his advisers handle the problem on his behalf and not bother him about it. This is probably the same reaction which more than 95% of readers would have if faced with the same set of circumstances. He might well have reasoned that the problems with Jeeves Dramatics were not of his making, rather they arose because of the initial shoddy administrative plan established by Rumsey, with whose services he had dispensed.

Nevertheless, Wodehouse wanted the position regularised as simply and quickly as possible — by a generic group of "his advisers". The difficulty which he faced was in fact exacerbated by his reluctance to accept the advice on this matter from Reynolds and his naive preference to revert to Denby for assistance. Relatively little is known about Denby, who had been Wodehouse's US agent before the move to Reynolds and appears to have been a close friend of Ethel, and at this time he retained some residual business connections with PG. In particular, he acted in connection with an attempt to have cancelled, in return for some compensation, a contract with *Famous Players*, and wrote on 13 January, 1927, that he would remit the $ 5,500 compensation that he had received to PGW's Hong Kong bank account. He added:

> If the money is dealt with in this way there will be no need for you to make mention of it in either British or American Tax returns.

The question of whether the payment should have been charged to tax would depend on a number of factors, but the bank account to which it was remitted is unlikely to have been one of them. As compensation for the termination of a contract, it is quite likely that the correct treatment for both UK and US tax purposes was to regard it as a capital gain, non-taxable to a non-resident. So it is not necessarily *WHAT* Denby says that makes one uneasy at his approach as much as *HOW* he said it.

And Denby's appointment opened the way for an even more questionable one. After recovering his health in summer 1931, one of his first actions according to the draft of a deposition which was prepared for him to sign, was to retain Messrs Freeman and Greenberg, who had been recommended to him as competent and reliable income tax experts. Greenberg was the individual who became involved, and proved to be one of the few human beings that Wodehouse actively disliked. Wodehouse actually questioned his honesty, in writing, not a course that he would often follow! And he was eventually removed from the assignment with a substantial outstanding fee, as will be described in chapter 5.

Within the scope of the responsibilities which he had at any time, Reynolds appears to have continued to be meticulous in his attention to record-keeping, even if minor matters were understandably permitted to lie around for some months before receiving attention. This is illustrated by a letter of 7 January, 1929, concerning two small sums which he he was remitting to Wodehouse and which had their origins in 1925 and 1926:

1   During 1925 Congress had passed a bill reducing the rate of Non-Resident Alien Income Tax from 6% to 5%. Reynolds had deducted a total of $ 338.54 at 6% from remittances in respect of Doran royalties, and Wodehouse was therefore entitled to a refund of 1%, ie $ 56.42.

2   The other item was $ 65.74, which was deducted from a remittance on 19 July, 1926. No further tax was deducted after the formation of Jeeves Dramatics, Inc. Reynolds felt that by 1929, there was no point in paying this over to the Government, so he returned it.

Finally, Paul Reynolds' greater awareness of his fiscal responsibilities to the Wodehouses after the events described in this chapter can be illustrated by two small pieces of correspondence in August 1930. In the first, Reynolds jnr says in a file note:

If any royalties come in for Wodehouse there is an income tax on royalties but not on the advance. In the past Mrs Wodehouse has told us to deposit such money to Jeeves Dramatics Inc and not to withhold the income tax, and you will have to ask my father whether he wants to do that or whether he wants to withhold the income tax and deposit to the Ethel and P G Wodehouse account.

Two days later, on 8 August, he wrote to Ethel at Culver City asking for instructions in relation to a payment of $256.40 that he had received on their behalf:

> I don't want Denby to say that I am making his course more difficult by paying money into Jeeves that ought not to go there, or I can, if you wish me to, retain 5% ($12.82) which is the tax on book royalties on a non-resident alien, and pay the money into the account of Ethel and P G Wodehouse.

As far as the Reynolds were concerned, therefore, everything was going to be all above board.

The 5% rate of tax mentioned can not by itself be regarded as penal. This seems to have been at least tacitly accepted by other non-residents who were enjoying the best that Hollywood had to offer in the years immediately after the crash. For example, Leslie Howard's daughter, L R Howard, wrote in *A Quite Remarkable Father*[1] in the following manner about the early 1930's:

> Despite the financial insecurity which haunted the country, people still went to the movies, and motion pictures were making more money than ever for the studios. While the rest of America dragged its hungry, weary way through the depression years, the gilded personalities of the celluloid empire enjoyed an era of low income-tax, high earnings and incredible spending.

Another artist whose professional achievements were reaching a high point during this period was the composer Irving Berlin, who was able to maintain a successful career almost as long as Wodehouse. According to Benny Green, in *Let's Face The Music*[2] (Pavilion Books, 1989), as the years went by and he did not follow his contemporaries to the grave, Berlin became the butt of jokes. He was said to be so rich that the government was paying *him* income tax, and cynics speculated that since he had been told that you can't take it with you, he had decided not to go.

And how had his growing problem with the tax authorities shown up in Wodehouse's written work during the seven-year period covered by this chapter? A hint was given in chapter 3 that one aspect of the **William Tell** story could be found later — in a stanza of the lyric *Bongo on the Congo*, which was written for *Sitting Pretty* in 1924:

In Bongo, its on the Congo
And boy, what a spot.
Quite full of things delightful,
And few that are not.
There no-one collars your hard-earned dollars,
They've a system that's a bear
When government assessors call
To try and sneak your little all
You simply hit them with an axe
Its how you pay your income tax
In Bongo, its on the Congo
And I wish that I was there.

In the same year he demonstrated his awareness of the tendency of certain types of citizen to use techniques of tax evasion rather than mitigation to reduce their taxes, although he was prepared to see those who so indulged get their come-uppance. The relevant scene, from **Bill The Conqueror**[3], has Judson Coker speaking to Bill Paradene West concerning the way in which he, Judson, had persuaded Roderick Pyke to leave the country and not marry Bill's intended, Felicia (Flick) Sheridan:

.....It turned out that, as far as the money end of it was concerned, he was sitting very pretty. Some time ago, in order to do down the income-tax people, old Pyke had transferred a large mass of wealth to this bird's account, the understanding being that Roddy — I was calling him Roddy by this time — was to return it in due season. "Be a man," I said. "Collar the cash, send a few wires of farewell and leg it for foreign parts." He burst into tears, clasped my hand and said that I was one of the master-minds of the age.

In the same book, he acknowledged the possibility of reducing future tax liabilities by entering into legally binding obligations which will only have a real impact at a later date. In this extract the relevant tax was inheritance tax, or death duty, which can be minimised by making outright gifts to other people. (Note that one of the enthusiasts for the notion that Mr Cooley may be about to make settlements, is Uncle Jasper. Any character in Wodehouse blessed with the name "Jasper" is immediately recognisable by the reader as too sharp for his own good, and destined for a future which, if not sticky, will be undoubtedly uncomfortable or embarrassing[4], although in the case of Sir Jasper ffinch-ffarrowmere, the name Jasper was a bluff, a deliberate attempt to mislead the reader into believing the worst.)

> "If you ask me," [Uncle Otis] said, "there's something in the wind. My idea is that Cooley probably realises that he's getting pretty old, so he's going to make settlements on us all."
>
> "Oh, do you really, really fink so?" exclaimed Cousin Evelyn rapturously. "Of course, he *is* old, isn't he? I always say that when a man has passed sixty he's simply waiting for the end."
>
> "I was sixty-two last birthday," said Uncle Otis coldly.
>
> "Settlements?" said Uncle Jasper thoughtfully. He scratched his chin. "H'm. Not a bad idea. Save us a lot of money on the inheritance tax."

Wodehouse will also refer to tax as a weapon used by the unscrupulous politician to keep down the proletariat, as in *The Long Arm of Looney Coote*[5]:

> [Corky has seen a political poster re Boko Lawlor.]

You could see at a glance that here was one who, if elected, would do his underhand best to cut down the Navy, tax the poor man's food, and strike a series of blows at the very root of the home.

His next two references to taxes tackled similar situations from opposite angles. The first, in **Came The Dawn**[6], showed his awareness that a considerable burden of responsibility might be perceived by the daughter of a peer made impecunious by the tax system. In Wodehouseland, her first thought would be to ignore her inner, finer, feelings and concentrate instead on the attractions of a suitor who had it:

[Lancelot Mulliner has met, and immediately proposed to, Angela, daughter of the Earl of Biddlecombe. She is impressed with his dancing, but is also conscious of the fact that his rival, presently leading the chase for her hand, would bring much-needed financial relief to the family.]

"Well, earls aren't everything," said Lancelot with a touch of pique. "The Mulliners are an old and honourable family. A Sieur de Moulinières came over with the Conqueror."

"Ah, but did a Sieur de Moulinières ever do down the common people for a few hundred thousand and salt it away in gilt-edged securities? That's what's going to count with the aged parent. What with taxes and super-taxes and death duties and falling land-values, there has of recent years been very, very little of the right stuff in the Biddlecombe sock."

This is the story in which the disastrous effects of high taxation are illustrated by attributing to Lord Biddlecombe a genius for invention which he puts to good, and commercial, use with such products as *Mouso-Penso*, a "combination mousetrap and pencil sharpener invented by Lord Biddlecombe, forced into commerce by recent legislation of a harsh and socialistic trend".

Needless to say, the tale culminates in the way the reader would expect.

In the second story, **The Ordeal of Osbert Mulliner**[7], Mr Mulliner speaks glowingly of the good fortune of his nephew:

> Fortune seemed to have lavished her favours on my nephew Osbert in full and even overflowing measure. Handsome, like all the Mulliners, he possessed in addition to good looks the inestimable blessings of perfect health, a cheerful disposition, and so much money that Income-Tax assessors screamed with joy when forwarding Schedule D to his address.

The first reference to taxes in the Jeeves saga comes in the 1930 story **Jeeves and the Kid Clementina**[8]. It shows a different slant again, this time the contempt of a taxpayer (a headmistress) for the ability of the authorities — represented by the police — to make good use of the tributes delivered to them by herself and her down-trodden fellows:

> "The officer is a fool," said Miss Mapleton. It seemed a close thing for a moment whether or not she would rap him on the knuckles with a ruler. "By this time, no doubt, owing to his idiocy, the miscreants have made good their escape. And it is for this," said Miss Mapleton, "that we pay rates and taxes!"

In 1926, Wodehouse and Guy Bolton wrote the book for a very successful George and Ira Gershwin musical comedy, **Oh, Kay!** The story was based on the then topical subject of bootlegging, but the plot involved, as chief bootleggers, the very English Duke of Durham (who evolved into the Earl of Blandings in the 1960 revival) and his sister, Kay. The plot was complicated by the unexpected return home of the hero, Jimmy Winter, and the antics of the two assistant bootleggers, Larry Potter and Shorty, who, in Jimmy's absence, had used the Winter home as a storage depot for the stuff.

Jimmy returns to find a number of unexpected guests calling at his home, including the Revenue Agent, Jansen, who wishes to arrest at least the Duke and Kay, but, increasingly, Jimmy as well. Jimmy, who is, of course, in love with Kay, is in the process of marrying Constance for the second time, but the ceremony is held up when Jansen seeks to arrest him, Kay and the Duke. Constance inevitably does not stand by Jimmy, which solves one personal problem; their escape from the clutches of the law is facilitated by the discovery that Jansen is actually not a Revenue agent but a hijacker, and his target is the Duke's goods.

Kay responds to Jimmy's overtures, and he confirms that her murky past holds no terrors for him:

Kay: Were you very shocked when I told you I
          was a bootlegger?

Jimmy: Not a bit.   Women are invading all the
          learned professions nowadays.

Kay: You see, what with taxes and super-taxes
          and inheritance taxes, all my brother had left
          was his yacht.

Jimmy: So he decided to do something really useful?
          Splendid.

There was an assumption that corruption was rife amongst those required to enforce the Prohibition laws, and jokes such as the following reflect this:

[The Revenue Officer is talking to Jimmy Winter and Shorty]

Rev Off.: Say, do you know why I joined the Revenue
          service?

Jimmy: I know — don't tell me, the stuff got too expensive to buy.

Shorty: Now I'll tell one. Do you know the difference between a revenue officer and a bootlegger?

Jimmy: Go ahead, I'll bite.

Shorty: One of 'em wears a badge.

This musical was very successful during its first run on both sides of the Atlantic, and again when it was revived in 1960, even though it was not universally liked by the critics.

At about this time, Wodehouse met W C Fields in Hollywood, and when writing about his experiences in **Bring on the Girls**[9] he put the following words into Fields' mouth:

"I was up late last night, seeing the New Year in. Yes, I am aware that the general consensus of informed opinion in these degenerate days is that the year begins on January the first — but what reason do we have for supposing so? One only ... that the ancient Romans said it did. But what ancient Romans? Probably a bunch of souses who were well into their fifth bottle of Falernian wine. The Phoenicians held that it began on November the twenty-first. The medieval Christians threw celluloid balls at one another on the night of March the fifteenth. The Greeks were broadminded. Some of them thought New Year's Day came on September the twentieth, while others voted for the tenth of June. This was good for the restaurateurs who could count on two big nights in the year, but confusing for the Income Tax authorities, who couldn't decide when to send in their demands."

The financial situation of the potential marriage-partners of Wodehouse's characters continued to give cause for concern to their parents and guardians almost throughout the Wodehouse oeuvre. Some, such as Sir Herbert Bassinger in **If I Were You**[10], might appear to the reader to be a little greedy in his aspirations for his former ward, Tony, 5th Earl of Droitwich:

> Sir Herbert [Bassinger] was appalled. As Earl of Droitwich, Tony would be quite comfortably provided with the world's goods, but by no means so well provided — what with Death Duties and Land Taxes and all the rest of it — as to be in a position lightly to sever relations with the heiress of Waddington's Ninety-Seven Soups.

There are two speeches in **Big Money**[11] which indicate what happens to an heir who hasn't been able to find a suitably wealthy heiress to help with the upkeep of the historic pile:

> *[Lord Biskerton, known as 'the Biscuit' is in conversation with his friend, Berry Conway, in each extract.]*
>
> "But I've always thought of you as rolling in money, Biscuit. You've got that enormous place in Sussex?"
>
> "That's just what's wrong with it. Too enormous. Eats up all the family revenues, old boy. Oh, I know how you came to be misled. The error is a common one. You see a photograph in *Country Life* of an Earl standing in a negligent attitude outside the north-east piazza of his seat in Loamshire, and you say to yourself, "Lucky devil! I'll make that bird's acquaintance and touch him." Little knowing that even as the camera clicked the poor old deadbeat was wondering where on earth the money was coming from to give the piazza the lick of paint it so badly needed. What with the Land Tax and the Income Tax and the Super Tax and all the

little Taxes, there's not much left in the family sock these days, old boy. It all comes down to this," said the Biscuit, summing up. "If England wants a happy, well-fed aristocracy, she mustn't have wars. She can't have it both ways."

And later, philosophising with some ingenuity about the solution to the problem of poverty, he reverts to the form of taxation preferred by Morton in mediaeval times:

"What ought to happen," said the Biscuit, "is this. If I had the management of this country, there would be public examinations held twice a year, at which these old crumbs with their hoarded wealth would be brought up and subjected to a very severe inquisition. "You!" the Examiner would say, looking pretty sharply at Frisby. "How much have *you* got? Indeed? Really? As much as that, eh? Well, kindly inform this court what you do with it." The wretched man, who seems to feel his position acutely, snuffles a bit. "Come on, now!" says the Examiner, rapping the table. "No subterfuge. No evasion. How do you employ this very decent slice of the needful?" "Well, as a matter of fact," mumbles old Frisby, trying to avoid his eye, "I shove it away behind a brick and go out and get some more." "Is that so?" says the Examiner. "Well, upon my Sam! I never heard anything so disgraceful in my living puff. It's a crying outrage. A bally scandal. Take ten million away from this miserable louse and hand it over to excellent old Biskerton, who will make a proper use of it. And then ask Berry Conway how much he wants." We'd get somewhere then."

Footnotes

1   1959, Longman
2   1989, Pavilion Books
3   1924, Methuen

4 Examples include:
   Sir Jasper Addleton, The Smile That Wins, in **Mulliner Nights**, 1933
      Herbert Jenkins
   Jasper Biffen, Big Business, December 13, 1952, Colliers
   Sir Jasper Todd, Big Business, in **A Few Quick Ones**, 1959, Herbert Jenkins
   Sir Jasper ffinch-ffarrowmere, A Slice of Life, in **Meet Mr Mulliner**, 1927
      Herbert Jenkins
5 **Ukridge.** 1924, Herbert Jenkins
6 in **Meet Mr Mulliner.** 1927, Herbert Jenkins
7 in **Mr Mulliner Speaking.** 1929, Herbert Jenkins
8 in **Very Good, Jeeves.** 1930, Herbert Jenkins
9 1954, Herbert Jenkins
10 1931, Herbert Jenkins
11 1931, Herbert Jenkins

CHAPTER 5: 1932 to 1936 — THE BITE IS ON

At the end of chapter 4, the tax affairs of the Wodehouses had been left at the mercy of Bobbie Denby, a doubtful privilege. Reynolds was obviously still heavily involved in Wodehouse's general business affairs as his US literary agent, and this would continue until Reynolds' death, but he had a less direct official role in the Wodehouse tax affairs. Early in 1932, though, he had to write to Wodehouse in France to tell him that Rumsey had been subpoenaed in connection with the tax affairs of Jeeves Dramatics, Inc.

Time moved inexorably onwards and the tax authorities in both the US and the UK started putting the bite on what must have seemed a very promising source of income. By the middle of 1932, Wodehouse was resigned to the fact that there would be a considerable sum owing to the US authorities, and had just been told that tax was owed in the UK as well.

And to make matters worse, progress on the US side was very slow. On 23 July, 1932, Denby wrote from Middleboro, Massachusetts, where he was staying with Cosmo Hamilton:

> The Greenberg business is going along — slowly but surely. As I told you before, it can't be hurried. It takes time to get copies of papers from bankers and brokers. And we shall be able to make a settlement more favourable to us if we wear the tax people down a bit.

A questionable strategy, when Wodehouse had been saying for two years that he wanted it settled, even at a high tax cost.

In a letter to Townend on 13 August, 1932, he expressed himself lucidly:

Hell's foundations are quivering a bit at the moment on account of vast sums to be paid out soon for both English and American income tax. The trouble about this income tax business is that if you simply pay you get soaked much too much, while if you engage a hired bravo to fight them on every point and contest every claim, you save a lot in the end but it means that you are suddenly informed that your income tax affairs dating from the year 1896 are now settled and will you kindly forward a cheque for about three thousand quid.

In America it's even worse. God knows how much I shall be made to pay there. Fortunately, in America you can keep a thing like that dragging on for ever and pay in instalments.

While in London for Leonora's wedding in November 1932, he met an English accountant, H E Wiltshire, who had gone to him with a new idea for reducing his tax bill. He wrote to Reynolds on 12 December, warning him that he was sending Wiltshire over to see him and said:

I have been a month in London, doing nothing but talk figures to an American income tax expert, who is trying to unravel the mess my affairs have got into over there! He has gone back now — you met him, I believe? Greenberg? I didn't like him at all, and am very dubious about his honesty.

In order to straighten things out, I am sending my English man over to New York on the 17th December — H E Wiltshire. I have asked him to call and see you, as it may be necessary with future contracts to have them made out not to me but to some third party, and I think of getting Newnes to take over all contracts for my stories ie you would make them just as before and handle all the business, but instead of the contract being between me and the magazine it would be between George Newnes and Co and the magazine ...

77

In a nutshell, the position is that in order to straighten out this American income tax affair, I don't want to be technically making any money in America.

(Wiltshire had in fact already been in contact with Reynolds, seeking information on Wodehouse's trips to the US to assist negotiations with the UK Revenue.)

Although Wodehouse had taken a rare personal dislike, rational or otherwise, to Greenberg, he noted with pleasure that Greenberg thought that the US tax liability could be reduced from a potential $ 187,000 to a more palatable $ 70,000. This was all explained in a letter to Townend dated 1 December, 1932, which again starts in a very aggressive mood:

> Hell's foundations have been quivering, and I have been tied up all the time with income tax agents.
>
> A very nasty wallop has recently hit the home. Denby *[Author's comment — it would be interesting to have known whether this was a deliberate or accidental failure of PG's memory. As shown in chapter 4, it was Reynolds who first drew the problem to his attention]* wrote to us some months ago from America saying that the income tax authorities there had started to make enquiries and told us the only thing to do was to put everything in the hands of a firm who would manage things for us. Then we were told the head of this firm must come over — at our expense! — to confer with our English man. Well, he arrived, and the first thing he did was inform us that we owed the dear old American govt $ 187,000!!!
>
> Well, after this shock, he rather gave us to hope that he could reduce this to about $ 70,000. Any way the devil of it is that we have had to sell at an average of about 30 all those shares we bought for about $ 300. When the smoke has cleared away, I shall have lost

about 150,000 quid *[Author's comment — "quid" is slang for pound sterling]* since 1929. The position now seems to be that we shall have a capital of 40,000 quid plus whatever we can save from the wreck in America. We have removed all our money from America so if there is any rot about their demanding huge sums we can sit tight over here and tell them to try and get it. Any way we always did have too much money, and a nest-egg of about 50,000 quid in gilt-edged securities is as much as anybody could want.

Also, to add to the silver lining, there is the fact that our English man has fixed up a deal with the British government by which we pay 5,000 quid up to about January 1936, which squares us entirely with them. We've just paid 1,500, so we can make all the money we want to here and we shall not have to pay any more than the remaining 3,500. And, as this covers all tax from about 1924, I think its pretty good, as we've already wiped out the 3,500 by transferring money from USA and making on the exchange.

but concludes rather limply and uncharacteristically:

As a matter of fact, in some ways I am not sorry this income tax business has happened. Everything was so easy for me. Before that I was getting a bit bored. I now spit on my hands and start sweating again, feeling that it really matters when I make a bit of money.

He underestimated the persistence of the UK authorities, however, and as will be seen, it was only to be a few more months before they came round again with the begging bowl.

He followed up his theme in another letter to Townend on the same topic dated 4 January, 1933:

Every day we had conferences with our English income tax man, and I couldn't get away. It ended in our sending him over to America! (Incidentally, he travelled on the Majestic and ran into the worst storm on record, so he must be cursing us.)

The final score is as follows: I have had to sell out at about twenty a million stocks I bought at 250 and higher. The money has been transferred from America to England and is now in an English bank, where the American authorities can't touch it. It amounts to about seventy thousand quid. A nice sum in itself, but the American income tax people are presently demanding about fifty thousand!

My scheme is to imitate dear old France — the only sensible country on earth — and sit tight. If they will settle at a reasonable figure, O.K. If not, not a penny do they touch. A jolly strong position. I am hoping they will settle for about six thousand quid.

Anyway, there it is.

What must have been the biggest shock of the whole investigation came with a telegram from Reynolds on 11 April, 1933:

Federal Tax Auditor in Annual Audit of our books found large payments to you and later informed us you had paid no taxes here. He said he proposed checking immediately your and Jeeves income here and assessing tax on total. Situation very serious. All future income in jeopardy. Understand Wiltshire has been kept fully advised of this possibility and Perkins Malone and Washburn have been awaiting retainer before proceeding.

That this seems to have generated an understanding that the situation was serious can be seen from his immediate and somewhat irritable response by letter to Reynolds on 12 April, the

80

tenor of which again suggests that Wodehouse was relying on his professional help to extract him from the soup in as painless way as possible, but had not been plotting dastardly schemes to cheat the IRS:

> Your cable was a bombshell. You speak of the authorities informing you of our non-payment of taxes as if it were a discovery. Surely the whole point of all this trouble we have been to for the last year or so — sending Wiltshire over to N.Y. etc — has been due to the fact that we knew we had not paid taxes and the authorities knew we had not paid taxes and that we wanted to pay them, and get the thing settled — for which reason we gave Wiltshire power of attorney which he handed to Malone and Washburn ...

> All I know is this: — Wiltshire told me on his return that he and Washburn had seen the authorities, who were quite willing to wait till we could assemble the figures — and that he had placed the whole business in W's hands & that they were working towards a settlement.

After a little more thought, Wodehouse erroneously and naively convinced himself that perhaps things weren't quite as bad as they might have been. He came up with the notion that he would be able to deduct his heavy stock exchange losses (incurred in 1929) in computing the bill, and suggested the possibility to Reynolds in a letter on 18 April, 1933:

> My wife is frightfully worried about this Income Tax thing, but personally, I can't see that it will be so bad, as my Stock Exchange losses were so big that, if — as is presumably the case — I am allowed to deduct these, there should be very little tax to pay. And, anyway, surely I can make an arrangement to work it off by giving the tax people — say half of whatever I make in America till further notice.

He also queried again whether one way out of a dilemma should remittances become difficult would be for the British publisher, Newnes & Co, to take over the Cosmopolitan contract, so that remittances would be payable to Newnes. This idea was squashed by Reynolds on 26 April. In the same letter, proving he had not totally been crushed by events he said:

> By the way, this ought to give you a laugh. Our friend Greenberg a few weeks ago was telling me to cable him $ 5,000 to square his account. He now says that he is willing to accept $ 500.

Reynolds would not let Wodehouse be under delusions about the likely outcome, even though he knew it was likely to damage their personal relationship, and was working hard to present a balanced picture to his irascible client. On 24 April he reminded Wodehouse that he had not been involved in the question of Wodehouse's taxes, having sent Wodehouse to see Mr Malone and his partner Mr Washburn. But he was able to explain that it was the New York State authorities who were aware of the problem, and the Federal Tax auditors who had "discovered" the problem during their audit of Reynolds books.

Two days later he was pleading with Wodehouse either to pay Malone the requested retainer or obtain other legal representation:

> You have Mr Malone now refusing to act until you pay him the amount he demands as a retainer, and you have no lawyer to represent you or to put your case before the people in Washington, and, as far as I can see it, you are running the risk of having to pay a tremendous amount, and, if an arrangement isn't made for payment of the taxes, the government, by restraining the magazines and book publishers from paying you any money, will simply prevent your getting any money from America.

Wodehouse, probably guilty of a knee-jerk reaction, and still very confused, sent a telegram demanding that all his assets be paid to his bank in London. Reynolds carried this out, even though he was potentially exposing himself to a charge of complicity. He covered the matter by cable and letter (27 April, 1933):

> Remitting all money to Barclay's despite our liability for taxes on book royalties or otherwise.
>
> Mr Malone advises us that by sending this money to you we might be held by the Washington Tax Authorities for entering into conspiracy with you to send money out of the country which should be paid to the tax authorities.
>
> According to the law, we are required to hold out the income tax from the book royalties. We did not do it with you because when we first started this practice, we thought your taxes were being taken care of in other ways ...

An ancillary problem was that Washburn had not started to act for Wodehouse as he had still not received the retainer. Wodehouse was furious with Wiltshire when he found out for, as he wrote to Reynolds on 2 May:

> He [Wiltshire] never told me there was any hitch about Washburn and the retainer....I am awfully sorry you have been given so much worry about this beastly tax business.

Meanwhile, Malone told Reynolds that there would be more chance of reducing a penalty in front of a civil court. But he [Malone] was afraid that Wodehouse's only fear was that the affair might leak into the papers. Reynolds declined to give an opinion on this idea to Wodehouse.

An interesting insight into the sums involved in book royalties (as opposed to advances) can be obtained from a letter from Reynolds to B A Acker, of Acker, Bacas and McGirl on 17 May, 1933:

The amount of the Income Tax withheld by us and paid to the government on P G Wodehouse from 1920 to 1925 was as follows:

	Am't of Roy	I.T. withheld
1920	32.12	2.57
1921	9.00	.72
1922	378.01	30.23
1923	872.44	69.79
1924	1,453.01	87.18
1925	5,417.71	270.88

Note that the rate of withholding declined from 8% in 1920 through 1923 to 6% in 1924 and 5% in 1925.

Washburn evidently made a proposal to Wodehouse around this time that they should seek to ignore the existence of Jeeves Dramatics Inc in view of that company's doubtful pedigree, and have Wodehouse pay back taxes as though he had personally received the amounts accruing to Jeeves Dramatics. But Wodehouse wrote to Reynolds on 15 June explaining most lucidly the trap that this course would create, and it is worth reproducing most of his letter:

In America my tax can be paid either by Jeeves Dramatics or by P.G.W. as an individual. If the former, the thing is straightforward — it is simply a question of how much the company owes in tax on my earnings assigned to it. But Washburn, being a smart lawyer, has suddenly spotted a flaw in the Tax Authorities case, due to the clause in the law which says that "articles manufactured out of the country" are not liable to tax, or words to that effect. And he thinks he sees a chance of scaling down my liabilities in America considerably by this means.

But mark what happens if he does. Wiltshire, after a terrific fight, got the English Income Tax people to admit that my earnings in America, being the property of Jeeves Dramatics, were not liable to tax in England. The assumption being, of course, that Jeeves Dramatics paid all American Income Tax.

Well, then, if Washburn comes along and shoves Jeeves Dramatics aside and establishes me in America as an individual tax-payer, this is fine as regards my American tax, but instantly the English tax people say "Oh, so P.G.W. pays American tax on his earnings. Well, he must pay English tax on it, too." And the result is that they reopen the matter for which Wiltshire got a settlement and soak me for English tax on the years 1926-1930 at a rate of about ten shillings in the pound.

You see what I'm driving at. Washburn may save me something on the swings by this scheme of his, but what good is that to me, as I shall lose double or treble on the roundabouts. I estimate that, if he establishes me as an individual payer in America, I shall be liable to about fifteen thousand pounds of tax in England.

So will you head him off. I've already cabled and written to him, but a word from you would make things clearer and it would also ease my mind.

That, by the way, is an important point. This tax matter, dragging along like this, is playing the devil with my work. I write a few pages and then along comes another letter from Washburn, full of disturbing stuff, and I find it impossible to go on with my story.

I wish you would take up with him the possibility of making an offer of some definite sum to the Tax people, so that I could pay it and be quit of the worry of all this uncertainty.

My wife says "But why should they settle, if they know they are bound to get what they want in the end?" Very true, too, only it is a fact that Tax authorities do make settlements. The English people did. Just the same arguments and delays went on over here for years, and then suddenly the thing collapsed and Wiltshire made an arrangement with them that I should pay five thousand pounds to cover all back demands and see me through till the end of 1934. That is to say, a nice sporting lump-sum deal, both sides satisfied.

Now, can't something like that possibly be fixed over in America? If they would agree to a fixed sum, then we on our side would agree to drop all haggling about expenses and losses and so on. I can't see why it isn't possible.

If this is not a plea for the professionals to get the matter sorted out so that he can get back to what he loved doing most, then it is difficult to see what could be! Wodehouse could write during his wife's parties and, looking forward to the 1940s, in a prisoner-of-war camp with ping-pong balls flying round his head, or in a mental hospital, but to work with the mental stress imposed by the tax authorities was impossible!

Reynolds replied sympathetically on 24 June, and agreed to speak to Washburn, following which he reported on 11 July that Washburn had made a number of further suggestions, but none appear to have been followed up.

Before material progress had been made on the negotiation of a settlement in the US, Wodehouse had another shock. The UK authorities, having apparently come to an agreement with him, read up on their Dickens and, like Oliver Twist, they came back for more. He explained the position to Townend in a letter of 7 December, 1933:

> I meant to write before but Hell's foundations have been quivering again. Out of a blue sky the English income tax authorities have just jumped on my neck in re non-payment of tax on my American earnings for the last five years! This necessitated endless conferences with accountants, etc. It looks as if the thing might straighten itself out fairly well now. The appeal is on Dec 18, and we seem to have a pretty good case. But my gosh, all this business has been the devil. I had been told that I was absolutely straight as regards English income tax, and was feeling happy because I had ceased to regard the American situation as important (!!).
>
> The English assessors started by demanding 40,000 quid from 1927 to 1933. A little cool reflection showed that they couldn't claim on 1930 to 33 as I was out of the country all the time. *[Author's comment — Something of an exaggeration, bearing in mind his presence at Leonora's wedding in November 1932.]* The snag is the years 1927 to 28 when I was a resident here, which involves about 12,000 quid. Our accountants seem to think the actual sum required will be a couple of thousand. Maybe less. Anyway we shall know shortly.

As is so often the case, there was an adjournment of one month before the case was heard, but Wodehouse's appeal against assessments (for the years 1927/28 through 1933/34) under Schedule D of the Income Tax Act 1918, in respect of literary earnings from contracts he made in America and assigned to Jeeves Dramatics, Inc., came before the Commissioners for the General Purposes of the Income Tax for the Division of St Martins-in-the-Fields in the County of London on 19 January, 1934.

He was represented by Raymond Needham, KC *[King's Counsel]* and there were two points at issue. The first was whether he was resident in England in the relevant years, and the second was whether he could legally assign his contracts for literary and dramatic works to a company. On the first point, it was submitted that the house in Norfolk Street was purchased, not for his own occupation, but for his step-daughter, who had let it furnished for the past three years and recently again for the next three. The Commissioners found first, he had only been resident in England in two of the seven years, and secondly, that he could legally assign his contracts to a company.

According to Richard Usborne (in the brief section entitled *Dedications* in **Vintage Wodehouse**[1]), the vanquished foe was a tax inspector who had been in charge of the Wodehouse UK tax file for a number of years, and was confident of success. Needham was the top practising tax barrister at the time, and when approached by Wodehouse's solicitors agreed to take the brief against the Revenue. The inspector, who turned out to be someone whom Needham had previously both represented and opposed, made a mistake in presenting the case, which Needham successfully seized on.

The furious inspector intended to appeal against the judgment, but Needham is reputed to have said:

"Well, anyway, come and have lunch with us now."

"Us? Who else?"

"My client, P G Wodehouse. Savoy Grill at one."

The inspector finally and grudgingly accepted and at the end of the lunch came out arm in arm with Wodehouse, having discovered that they were on opposing sides in a school rugger match, *Dulwich v Bedford*, in the late 1890's. But it probably was for a different reason that the decision was not ultimately appealed by the Revenue! So his clash with the UK authorities had a successful outcome — Wodehouse stood up for his rights, and was not going to be bullied by a bureaucracy. That should have put the US authorities on their guard, and sent a message to them that they attacked P G Wodehouse at their peril!

The real importance or otherwise of the decision to the tax authorities can be gauged from the delay of 35 years which occurred before the tax effectiveness of assigning contracts to companies in the UK was reduced by new legislation in 1969. One really has to question whether the problem of this sort of assignment was really of such importance to the Revenue in 1933 for them to take a case through the Courts, if it was then decided that the law did not need to be changed for a generation! Whilst the residence issue was perhaps more relevant to Wodehouse's overall tax position, that was primarily a matter of fact rather than law, which it should have been possible to resolve without recourse to formal proceedings.

To publicly acknowledge his debt to Needham, Wodehouse wanted to dedicate his next book, **Right Ho, Jeeves**[2] to him. According to Usborne, Needham remembered the proposed dedication as something like:

> *To Raymond Needham, K.C., who put the*
> *tax-gatherers to flight when they had*
> *their feet on my neck and their hands*
> *on my wallet.*

Needham warned that this would infuriate the Revenue and make the inspector open the file again. So the dedication was cut as rigorously as Wodehouse cut his best stories, and all that is left is:

> *To*
> *RAYMOND NEEDHAM, K.C.*
>
> *WITH AFFECTION AND ADMIRATION*

The dedication did not appear in the US equivalent, **Brinkley Manor**, since the name would have meant absolutely nothing to his US readers.

Wodehouse was not slow in telling his friends of his success — he wrote to Reynolds on 25 January, 1934:

> You will be glad to hear that I won the case at this end. The English Authorities were trying to get £ 42,000 for tax on my earnings in America for 1927 on, and the Commissioners gave their decision in my favour, holding that as an individual I had nothing in America, the money being the property of Jeeves Dramatics, Inc. You can imagine what a relief it was.

And to Leonora:

> Mummie says will you send Needham a telegram congratulating him — just a short line ... I know he would appreciate it, and he has been wonderful ... Even now, I can't see how he worked the thing. Looking back to the case on Jan 19th, I see him proving us non-residents for years when — I should have said — we were out of England for about three days.

The English case increased his awareness of the need carefully to ration his time in England if he wanted to continue to minimise UK taxes. He wrote to Townend as early as 10 March, 1934 to say:

> My income tax experts tell me I have got to leave England, if only for a short spell, before April 5th. Otherwise I shall get chalked up as a resident.

By 27 March he understood more about the implications, and told Reynolds:

My plans are very uncertain. To establish non-residence (English) for income tax purposes I have to be out of England before April the 5th. My wife will stay on, as my daughter is having a baby some time in April [actually, March 31]. She will then join me, and we may stay at Cannes for the Summer or travel....I am very anxious to be in a position to go to America again as my wife and I both want to make it our headquarters. We both feel we have had enough of England except for occasional visits. What we would like would be to settle in America and visit the South of France from there in the Summer.

But when he wrote to Olive Grills (a friend known as Bubbles), on 26th April, 1934, he said, in a somewhat pained manner:

I have to be out of England for a year owing to some income tax technicality ...

and on 12 September, halfway through his full year of exile, he wrote to Townend:

This has been my worst year since I started writing — not in money, but in general discomfort of mind and feeling at a loose end. Not being able to come to England is a curse. I shall be glad when April comes.

The successful interlude with the tax authorities in the UK was pleasant, but it demonstrated the truth of the old saw, "One swallow does not make a summer". Wodehouse became increasingly frustrated with the time the US case was taking, as it restricted his freedom of action, as he saw it, not only as far as travel to and working in the US is concerned, but also in relation to the publication of stories, serials and books in the US.

Towards the end of 1933, or in early 1934, both Reynolds and Denby were asked to sign depositions prepared by Mr Malone to the effect that Wodehouse was entirely ignorant on the question of American taxes and that he had been badly advised as to how to deal with such taxes and this was the cause of the trouble into which he had got.

The scope of his problems in the US had widened beyond that of Jeeves Dramatics Inc., as the IRS had decided to investigate the tax position not only of the company, but Wodehouse himself, and the period under enquiry covered the years 1925 to 1931. Because of the length of time that the review — and the negotiation of a settlement — took, it ended up covering the years 1932 and 1933 as well.

Wodehouse told Reynolds on 25 January, 1934, that his lawyer had returned from America the previous day, and reported that the decision on the American claim was held up and may be held up for quite a time. "Whatever happens I am hoping we shall be able to arrive at a compromise." But his tax advisers were less certain than he was that to make an offer would be good strategy. For instance, after Wodehouse wrote in a letter of 27 March:

> Also, I have had a contract offered me for one of those big musical comedies which mean such a lot of money, so I want to be in a position to be in America in the Fall ... Talking about income tax, I wish, if you see Washburn, Perkins, Malone, you would sound them as to the advisability of trying to settle my American tax muddle with an offer of a sum. I believe they are hard against it until we hear what the final assessment is. It is now three months since the case was heard.

Reynolds replied on 6 April:

> I have talked to Mr Malone about trying to settle the American tax muddle with the offer of a specified amount. I judge Mr Malone thinks this would be a great mistake, but he is going to talk it over with Washburn and let me know what they think. I of course explained your desire to have the matter settled. ....

Since writing the above I have talked with Mr Malone again and he says they have put up certain legal questions to the Solicitor-General and they expect an answer to those questions at any time. They feel very strongly that to make an offer of settlement at this time would severely weaken their position and that it would be a great mistake....They hope that the matter might be settled by the autumn and if that proves to be the case you would then be able to come over here in the autumn and in that way fulfil your present plans.

And also at this time Wodehouse entered into new arrangements — more complex than Jeeves Dramatics, Inc — designed to save taxes, once again through the use of a company. This time the company was to be based in Switzerland, and is referred to throughout this book as SwissCo. Washburn, whose idea it was, took the precaution of checking with Reynolds that editors and publishers would not object to making contracts with a Swiss corporation. He replied that, as long as they were getting a story written by PGW, they would not care whether they bought it from a corporation or Wodehouse. Reynolds's memo recording the conversation with Washburn noted that the principal purpose was to avoid Wodehouse having to pay surtax (also known as supertax) in England should he again become resident there. (It is interesting to note that within two years, when it became clear that Wodehouse had no immediate intention of returning to live in the United Kingdom, Washburn's partner, Malone, was calling SwissCo a liability.)

He announced the birth of this bouncing baby to Reynolds in joyful tone in a letter on 22 April:

Enclosed some formal stuff, designed to baffle the Income Tax sharks!

With that letter he sent the Reynolds agency a formal notice to the effect that all earnings, copyrights, royalties, commissions and other revenues on the sale of literary, theatrical or cinematographic productions had been sold to SwissCo for a period of four years from 25 April, 1934, to 24 April, 1938, and that all payments due should be sent to that company.

Reynolds received a call from Malone at the end of May 1935, with an estimate of the tax on Wodehouse's income for 1933 as about $ 11,000, a quarter of which would be due on June 15. He noted that Malone considered it would be a very good thing for Wodehouse to pay this tax "as far as the people in Washington are concerned".

The Wodehouse correspondence continued to commentate on developments, or more accurately the lack of developments, in his US tax position. On 11 June, 1934 he wrote to Townend:

> I've just sent my accountant Weinbren to New York to try to fix things. Ghastly expense, but worth it, I think ... I am saying they must be reasonable or they won't get anything.

By August he was again trying to find brightspots. To Townend on the 2nd:

> I sent Weinbren to America to fix the income tax thing. He wrote a triumphant letter saying he had got them to accept £ 6,000 instead of the £ 70,000 they are asking for, and we were frightfully bucked. Now comes a cable that says it has all fallen through and he is coming home. I don't know what can have gone wrong. Damned nuisance, as now I can't go to America.

Matters moved rapidly after Weinbren's failure, and Reynolds sent a telegram on 10 August, 1934:

Government has issued liens to us, editors, publishers and Metro — stop — No money can be paid to Washburn legally by us.

The lien — a later example of which is illustrated on page 138 — was issued on 8 August and refers to outstanding taxes for the period 1925-31. It claimed a debt totalling $ 250,703.59, representing tax of $ 123,826.00 and penalties of $ 126,877.59. This lien gave the IRS a charge over funds due to Wodehouse from those to whom it was sent, including for example Paul R Reynolds & Son and the publisher Dodd, Mead & Co. The lien prevented payment being made to PG or Ethel Wodehouse, but it was only after Reynolds took legal advice that he interpreted it as additionally applying to payments being made by him to SwissCo.

Reynolds wrote to Wodehouse on 9 August to express the hope again that the matter with the tax authorities could be settled in some satisfactory way. He suggested that in the meantime, if Wodehouse decided to have stories published in England he might send copies to Reynolds, who could have them printed in pamphlet form and sent for copyright approval to Washington. He agreed, though, that higher prices would be obtained if American publication were prior to English publication.

Wodehouse went into more detail about his disappointment in a letter of 16 August to Townend:

> Things aren't so bad as they seem at first sight, always provided that the English income tax people don't reopen that case which I won before the Commissioners in January. If they do, and win it, I may be soaked for a pretty good sum. But if they don't, I am in a pretty sound position. I have between 90,000 and 100,000 quid salted away in England and I have always earned in England hitherto about 8,000 or 9,000 a year. So I propose to sit tight and do nothing. Of course, the American authorities could stop me earning money in America under my own name, but if they do they won't get a cent, so I am inclined to think that eventually they

will compromise. Weinbren, my accountant, whom I sent over to America to fix things, cabled that he had argued my case before the Penal authorities and they agreed to settle for 6,000 quid cash. He asked the head of this gang what exactly this meant — did it mean that we had — say — a 50% chance of getting this agreement passed the higher board, and he said we had a 99% chance and gave Weinbren to understand that the ratification of the settlement would be a mere formality.

Imagine our feelings, then, when we got a later cable from Weinbren, saying that the higher board had flatly refused a settlement and he was coming home.

What happened in between those two meetings I can't imagine. The situation was almost as if an editor had accepted a story and named the price and then been overruled by his directors — ie almost impossible.

Well that didn't worry me too much, because I said to myself Weinbren told them we would think it over and make another offer, so I shall have at least six months before they turn nasty, during which six months I could shoot in a serial and six short stories. Then suddenly this thing happened. It is a complete mystery.

Meanwhile my lawyer in America is going to Washington to make another offer, and we are hoping for the best ... I do not know yet if the authorities have any power to stop payments on a story by me being made to a company. Any way, I'm full of buck and am prepared to fight it out by trench warfare for years. I feel that if I let two or three years go by and they see that I can hold out they will accept the compromise.

I feel very vicious against them, as they have behaved like bandits. They fined me 25% for not making a return and on top of that 75% for making a false return.

Now, how anyone can make a false return without making a return at all is a thing that seems to me to need explaining. However, I fancy the whole thing is largely bluff. They know that I have had offers to go to Hollywood, and they reason that I will do anything rather than give up these. Little knowing that I don't want to go to Hollywood at all. So long as my English market holds out, I am all right.

Following this freezing of his resources, Wodehouse cast around for ways to get round the difficulty. One idea — never fully developed — was to arrange for Newnes, the UK publisher, to buy rights and receive payments. Another, about which Wodehouse got quite animated, would have led to him publishing under a pen-name in the US (shades of **Not George Washington**[3], and his many articles for **Vanity Fair**). A further extract from the 16 August letter to Townend:

In a way the excitement of the thing rather dims the financial loss, though I am afraid Ethel is worried. I feel as if I am starting a new life. I can now send stuff to America without having to make it exactly like all my other stories. It will be rather fun seeing if I can build up another name.

That this was no idle threat can be illustrated by tracing the origin of the story **Reggie and the Greasy Bird**, published in the **Saturday Evening Post** on November 28, 1936[4]. This tale was originally written as a Drones Club tale, involving Freddie Widgeon, Lord Blicester, et al, with the title **The Masked Troubadour**, and was eventually published in the **Strand** in December 1936[5]. Because of the lien problem in the US, he rewrote the story with wholly new characters, and in a different setting, so that the writing might not be instantly recognised as Wodehouse. Under the title **Reggie and the Greasy Bird**, he submitted the revised story to the Saturday Evening Post, by whom it was accepted.

Ironically, by the publication date, the tax dispute was over, and the story actually appeared under Wodehouse's own name, but in its specially disguised form. It was admittedly not as good as the original — he said of it to Townend:

> I heartily concur with your remarks about *Reggie and the Greasy Bird*. In that shape, rotten.

Because Wodehouse was suddenly facing difficulties in getting paid for stories in the US from his traditional sources, his agents started looking elsewhere, although inevitably they were not prepared to pay the same price. On 31 August, Reynolds reminded Wodehouse that Mrs Meloney, Editor of the *This Week* supplement to the *New York Herald Tribune*, had offered $ 10,000 for a serialised story (**Laughing Gas**), and had said they would pay for it from their Paris office. This offer was accepted and led to some excited correspondence from a delighted PGW.

For example, the following letter, to Leonora (quoted in *Yours, Plum*[6], dated 18 October, 1934):

> I have just finished that story I told you about, the one where the chap's soul goes into the child star's body. It has come out magnificently, after a good many anxious moments. Ma Meloney, the editress of the NY Herald Magazine is giving me $ 10,000 for it (good sugar) and is having the Paris NY Herald pay me, thus utterly baffling the USA tax people and making them look pretty silly.

He boasted of the same idea to Townend in a letter of 15 October.

On 16 October the IRS wrote to Reynolds, a threatening sort of letter of which Roderick Spode and his Blackshorts might have been proud:

> *On August 8, 1934, we served you with notice of Tax lien for $ 250,703.59 against any funds due to P G Wodehouse and Ethel Wodehouse jointly and severally.*

Demand is hereby made for the above amount or any fraction thereof due to the above taxpayer.

Reynolds was able to reply that all the monies had gone to SwissCo.

But the issue of the liens had brought the matter to the public attention. In case its readers had missed it, *Cosmopolitan* included the following introduction to the story *Goodbye To All Cats* in November 1934:

> We have read that Uncle Sam says Mr Wodehouse owes $ 123,826 in income taxes. If he were taxed for all the laughs he has given us, he'd owe — oh! there isn't that much money in the world! Read this story and agree!

Wodehouse was now resigned to the situation. On 16 November he wrote to Townend:

> The American tax business has become comic. They are demanding $ 300,000, and my accountant, having gone into the figures, has written to the Federal Authorities offering them 1,500 quid in full settlement. I must say the Federal Authorities seem loony to me. They want to charge 50% penalty for making a false return and 25% penalty for not making a return at all. As we have pointed out to them, no, James, my boy, you cannot have both, you must choose between them. Also they charged me for profits on stock transactions but won't deduct losses.
>
> Of course the cardinal point (which we haven't yet broken to them, as it is so near Christmas and we don't want to spoil it for them) is that they can't get a cent if I don't choose to give it to them. My attitude has now become rather like that of a whimsical parent — shall I do the generous, though foolishly indulgent, thing and let them have a couple of hundred quid or so, or shall I say no you shall have nothing because you are greedy.

And anyway, what's the good of money to America at this stage? They are about 500bn in the red, so my little bit can't make any difference. Besides, they would only spend it.

Progress remained slow. Wodehouse told Leonora on 12 November:

> Our NY lawyer cabled us that he was having a conference with the income tax people last Saturday, but we have heard nothing since.
>
> I have nearly finished my novel, but I don't see how I am going to release it until this tax thing is settled.

and made the same point to Townend on the 17th ("I still can't get any answer from those USA tax people").

After finishing **The Luck of the Bodkins**[7] at the end of November, Wodehouse evidently felt the strain, commenting to Townend that he felt as though he were in a coma. He went on to say:

> As a matter of fact, my present collapse is the result of a strain that has gone on now for about six months. While in the middle of the novel and just beginning to see my way through it, I had to break off to start plotting out a musical comedy for New York with Howard Lindsay, the Producer. We toiled all through that blazing weather in Paris, and then we came down here and started all over again with Guy Bolton. In the end we got out a plot, and I wrote it — frightful sweat! — and sent it off to Guy to polish.
>
> While this was going on the American tax people put that lien on my money so I had to work with the feeling that I was probably not going to be able to collect my royalties.

The musical comedy to which he referred was **Anything Goes**, for which Cole Porter wrote the lyrics. But before the show could go on, the plot — involving a shipwreck — was overtaken by a real life disaster, with loss of life, and the book had to be rewritten. As Wodehouse and Bolton were not available to undertake this revision sufficiently quickly, it was handled by Howard Lindsay and Russell Crouse. Wodehouse said afterwards that they left about two lines of his in it "and so far I am receiving £ 50 a week apiece for them. That's about £ 3 10s a word, which is pretty good payment, though less, of course, than my stuff is worth."

A week later, he was back in inventive mood with another idea to beat the lien, again in a letter to Townend:

> It is so easy to get to England. The only trouble is that the pound is worth about ten bob in France now. E Phillips Oppenheim tells me that this is the reason he is leaving the Riviera.
>
> By the way, the American tax people are after him now. It certainly cuts both ways having an American market.
>
> I am reliably informed that if you sell your American rights to an English firm, the American authorities can't stop them selling it in America. So what I have to say is all I have to do is send Pop Grimsdick a cheque for a plausible amount — he cashes it and sends me a cheque for the same amount. Result so far — he is out tuppence and so am I. *[Author's comment — In England at the time there was a stamp duty of tuppence — two old pence; less than 1p in today's coinage — on the issue of a cheque.]* Then I cash his cheque and he has the cancelled cheque to show that the thing is a genuine sale, and then he goes ahead. I don't see how they can get round that.

Fortunately, there is no evidence that Wodehouse put into operation any of these more bizarre ideas for avoiding the lien. Although they were not related to the avoidance or evasion of tax as such, being merely concerned with maintaining a cashflow from sales of his work, the concept described in this letter relied on concealment and deception, and would certainly have been on the black rather than the white side of the dividing line.

The enforced year abroad and the related strain also affected his relationship with Leonora. On 19 December he wrote to her:

> I must say Le Touquet in winter, if you are all alone, is a quiet sort of spot. I would have liked it better, only I have just finished eight months of terrific strain, what with doing the novel, the novelette and the play and having all the income tax stuff as well, and I couldn't settle down to anything. I felt very let-down and at a loose end, and would love to have had a couple of weeks in London. I feel better now, and am getting ahead with some short stories. But I shall be glad when April comes and I can come over to England.

The evidence certainly supports the view that he was taking seriously the need to stay out of the UK for the whole tax year, and not to risk surreptitious visits to England to see Leonora, Townend or his other friends. He confirmed to Townend in a letter dated 6 March, 1935, that

> I shall come to England as soon after April 5 as I can manage.

It is also evident that the dispute with the tax authorities had made Wodehouse more anxious than normal about placing his material. Hence this further extract from the letter of 6 March:

> I am on tenterhooks about the fate of some stuff I sent over to New York. I got a letter from my agent saying that the editor of **The Red Book** liked the stories, but that a snag had arisen in the shape of the president of the company, which also owns **McCall's**, because in 1922 I contracted to do six short stories for **McCall's** and never delivered them! The president has been brooding on it ever since, and my agent says it rather

looks as if he may have to shade our price a bit as compensation.

Well, as anything I get out of America nowadays with this income-tax dispute going on is like a bone sneaked from a dog, I cabled "Close deal at any price you can get and cable at once." A telegram arrived that night. It was from Gertie Miller at Le Touquet, thanking me for having exercised her Dalmatian dog in her absence.

At about the same time there is clear evidence that Reynolds' involvement with Wodehouse's affairs had become more distant. Reynolds no longer acted as his agent, and wrote to Dr Paukner, who acted for Ladislaus Fodor, on 19 March 1935, in connection with *Good Morning, Bill*[8]:

As I have told you in conversation, Wodehouse has become involved with the tax authorities and our lawyers have advised us that we can act as advisers to Wodehouse but not as his agents.

A more detailed explanation is given in a letter to Reynolds dated 3 April:

Little Brown & Co and Doubleday Doran are apparently confused as to why my work is now being handled in America by the American Play Company and not by you.

I no longer possess any interest or control over the copyrights and sales of any stories bearing my name in America as I have sold out to SwissCo all my existing work and am under contract for a stated period to give them my products.

You are unable, apparently, to make payment to SwissCo I am told by that Corporation, because they say you will regard the lien placed on my property as having some relation with them and so they are obliged to take the selling of their property out of your hands.

103

The style of the letter, coupled with its unusual precision, accuracy and semi-technical language, makes it clear that the text was provided to Wodehouse by one of his advisers. Reynolds' response was friendly, understanding and constructive, expressing the hope that in due course things would return to normal (as indeed they ultimately did.)

With no progress having been made by the end of the year, Wodehouse started getting fidgety again. He wrote to Reynolds on 29 November:

> The tax business still drags on. I have very nearly given up hopes of a settlement, and am going to suggest to SwissCo that they sell world rights of my stories to the *Strand* magazine. The US authorities cannot, I believe, hold up money from an English firm which has bought world rights.

Nevertheless, the correct procedural form continued to be rigorously followed in relation to the business activities of SwissCo. The typed copy of *The Inside Stand* which was submitted for censorship approval on 19 October, 1935, prior to its London opening shows clearly on the front:

Property of:	Copyrighted in US by:
SwissCo	SwissCo
Zurich	Pelikanstrasse 2
Switzerland	Zurich Switzerland

Wodehouse remained clearly aware of the purpose and importance of SwissCo. During 1936 he engaged in correspondence with Mr McIntyre, of Little Brown, concerning the termination of his relationship with them and his return to the Doubleday fold. The letter he wrote on June 19, 1936, reproduced on page 105, is generally illustrative of the commercial approach he took to his writing business, and the last paragraph explains SwissCo's position.

June 19. 1936

Dear McIntyre.

I am most awfully sorry that there should have been any unpleasantness about this Doubleday contract, and especially that owing to Rumsey's negligence you should have received no reply to your letter suggesting a new contract.

But you must have misunderstood Weinbren if you got the impression that there was any pique or resetnment on our side.

The whole thing has been a perfectly straight business matter. Your publishing of my last three books was simply an experiment. The idea was that I was to receive reduced royal--ties and get increased sales, but it has not worked out that way. The sales of my last three books have been a good deal smaller than of those published by Doubleday. So now I am back as before.

I could understand Doubleday feeling aggrieved at my leaving him after he had published all my books in America except the first one or two, but your deal was definitely a limited one. You contracted for three books, which I delivered, and I cannot see why I should be supposed to be obligated beyond the terms of the contract

Exactly the same thing happened on this side. After publishing for many years with Jenkins, I signed a contract for three books with Methuen. When those three books had been printed, I returned to Jenkins. There was never any question of hurt feelings with Methuen about it.

S * is a business concern. When it has two offers, one of 15-17 and a half-20% on novels and the same on short story volumes and another of a flat 15% on novels and seven and a half on short story volumes, it naturally takes the former, the advance royal being the same in each case.

With best wishes

Yours sincerely

P.G. Wodehouse

* ie, the company referred to throughout the book as Swissco

Letter to **Little Brown**, the US publisher, concerning the termination of their contract.

The impasse between Wodehouse's advisers and the tax authorities lasted for something over a year. Marie Meloney, editor of the **This Week** section at the **New York Herald Tribune**, went to see the Secretary of the Treasury to try and generate some movement, and Wodehouse acknowledged his appreciation by letter on 25 May, 1936:

> It was awfully good of you to go to the Secretary of the Treasury about my tax business.
>
> I cannot understand the delay in at least giving a decision on my compromise offer — which they have had before them since August, 1934 ...
>
> I had a cable from Mr Washburn a week ago, saying that he expected a decision soon. This would encourage me more if I did not remember that in August 1934 he cabled me saying that he expected a decision within a month! I am perfectly willing to pay a reasonable sum in compromise. All I want them to do is say what they consider a reasonable sum. This thing of keeping my offer before them and taking no notice of it is maddening.

The Reynolds firm needed no third party to tell them of the effect the lien was having on Wodehouse's US market, but they received stark confirmation when Reynolds Jnr visited George Lorimer, Editor of **The Saturday Evening Post** in early June 1936. Lorimer made it clear that he would have bought Wodehouse's last story if it hadn't been for the tax difficulty.

Wodehouse had always had a good relationship with Lorimer, and bridges were repaired when the lien was removed, as outlined in an anecdote from a letter of 7 November, 1936, to Townend, concerning their first meeting on returning to the US:

> Before starting for California, I went to Philadelphia to see Lorimer. He was very friendly. Rather funny, when he bought '**The Crime Wave at Blandings**' after I had

had nothing in the **SEP** for a couple of years owing to my American income-tax trouble, he paid me $ 2,000 and wrote me a letter asking if that was all right. I wrote back: "Dear Mr Lorimer. I am so intensely spiritual that money means nothing to me, but I must confess that that $ 2,000 was a bit of a sock on the jaw, as I had always thought that a short story was supposed to fetch a tenth of the price of a serial, so I had been looking forward to $ 4,000." This apparently touched his heart, for the first thing he said to me when I came into his room was that he would pay $ 4,000.

When the breakthrough came, such was the high public profile both of Wodehouse himself and the tax problems of transatlantic authors, that the first news Reynolds had was from the press. He immediately cabled to Wodehouse, on 12 August 1936:

HOLLYWOOD PUBLICATION REPORTS YOUR TAX SETTLED.

Readers will recall that Wodehouse's strategy had been to keep out of the US for a couple of years, pay nothing, and try to have the IRS accept a compromise, as in that way they would get something. Well, perhaps the IRS had decided that it was running a bit short after all, because that press report was confirmed in a gleeful letter to Townend later in August:

And now for a great piece of news. My tax business has been settled. The Secretary of Treasury has signed, and all is well. You can imagine the relief.

and on 26th in a response to Reynolds' letter:

My settlement with the Gov^t was for $ 75,000 plus some $ 8,000 already held up by the Gov^t. This was Doubleday money and an advance on one Little Brown.

In that same letter, there appeared another interesting comment. A little earlier Reynolds had told Wodehouse that Mr Malone thought from a US point of view SwissCo may be a liability rather than an asset. Now, Wodehouse was in a position to use Reynolds as his agent once again, and he wrote:

> I shall bring over with me three short stories for you to place. I'm afraid it will have to be done for SwissCo, though, as you say, the thing is a liability. I can't get free from it until April 1938. You see, the US government may think SwissCo is fishy, but it is a perfectly genuine company, with which I have nothing to do — except, of course, that they listen to what I have to say as regards marketing stuff, and I have sold all my output to them for a period of four years, starting April 1934.
>
> The idea originally was to save super-tax if I wanted to live in England. But I prefer France, and I imagine that being domiciled in France [Author's comment — he almost certainly never was, at least in a technical UK tax sense — see the Appendix] I am not liable to English super-tax anyway...

And he summarised his feelings about the whole affair quite succinctly in a letter to George Lorimer, on 27 August:

> The period since the lien was put on my money in U.S.A. — August, 1934 — has been pretty much of a nightmare, and you will find me a bit aged from the carefree youth who washed the dishes at your farm in 1915. It was the slowness of it all that got on one's nerves. Even after the thing was practically settled, something like two months elapsed before the Secretary of the Treasury put his signature to the papers.

Two months later, in October, Wodehouse was back in Hollywood, and on 12 November 1936 Reynolds received a very formal confirmation from the Treasury Department that the lien had been withdrawn:

Reference is made to a notice of tax lien filed with you on August 8, 1934 in the amount of $ 250,703.59 against any property in your possession belonging to P G & Ethel Wodehouse.

You are advised that the above-mentioned lien is hereby withdrawn.

The withdrawal of the lien brought back Wodehouse's appreciation of his market value. Despite the service which Marie Meloney had performed, she was not going to receive unduly favourable terms for future stories, now that he once again had the whole of the American magazine market as his potential customers. His view was, if *Saturday Evening Post* will pay $ 3,500 for a short story such as **Anselm Gets His Chance**, and **Red Book** will pay $ 3,000, why should he let **This Week** have it for $ 2,000, let alone for the $ 1,000 he was forced to take for **Buried Treasure**, when he had to be grateful for what he could get. He would be prepared to take $ 2,500 from Mrs Meloney, but would prefer not to.

Anselm appeared in **The Saturday Evening Post** in July 1937.

The final piece of correspondence in this eon demonstrates Wodehouse's ongoing concern about his tax position. He wrote to Lorimer on 2 December:

My legal sharks tell me that it may complicate my English income tax position if I send my stuff direct to you, so I have mailed a couple of short stories — **ALL'S WELL WITH BINGO** and **ROMANCE AT DROITGATE SPA** — to Reynolds to send to you.

A rational person, reading the correspondence in this chapter for the first time, would undoubtedly conclude that Wodehouse had not sought to act illegally in his dealings with the tax authorities. He had appointed a range of advisers whom he assumed were competent, he had urged settlement of the dispute even before it started, and it would be disingenuous to assume that he was

109

writing some of the comments which appeared in his letters for the consumption of future generations of critics. He clearly believed SwissCo to have been genuine, for example, and carried on using it even when it apparently became a liability.

So again, when the time has come to return to look at his contemporary works, it is without having found any matter of note with which to quibble in his handling of his tax affairs, other than, possibly, indecisiveness in the exercise of supervision over his advisers.

But before moving totally away from the evolution of events during this period, it is worth stopping to consider briefly first, the tax position of one of Wodehouse's contemporary authors and fellow-contributor to many magazines, E Phillips Oppenheim, and secondly the way in which his close friend Guy Bolton reacted to the long-drawn out commentary on his tax problems.

An Englishman like Wodehouse, Oppenheim had also built himself a transatlantic market, and came up against the same harsh tax system. His biographer, Robert Standish, devoted a whole chapter to tax problems in *The Prince of Storytellers*[9]. The following extracts demonstrate that the incidence and levels of taxation were dear to his heart also, being instrumental in his decision to live first in France, and later, after he had realised the death duty implications of staying in France too long, in Guernsey (though this explanation does not agree with PGW's recollection):

> ... it is quite evident that as long ago as 1919 ... he was enormously concerned about his own taxes. There was in vogue at that time the iniquitous and wholly unfair system of double taxation which meant, in effect, that an author was taxed in America on his American earnings and then, without any relief of any kind, taxed at the prevailing rate of tax and surtax on the balance in England.

When he migrated to France this was one of the contributory reasons ... At that time France had a most liberal attitude to foreigners living in France whose incomes were derived from sources wholly outside France, so that French taxes were negligible. From that time onwards Phillips Oppenheim continued to pay his full taxes in England on what he earned in England and his full taxes in the US on what he earned there. From start to finish there was never the smallest flavour of illegality about anything he did in regard to taxes ...

There can be no question whatever that in his attitude towards the payment of taxes Phillips Oppenheim was always strictly within his rights. What is, however, much more interesting is to speculate as to whether, towards the end, if he had his life to live again he would have allowed tax considerations to influence his life quite as much as he did. In going to France to live he undoubtedly saved himself some thousands of pounds annually in Surtax, but it would seem, in retrospect, that he paid too high a price, for he forfeited so many things whose price cannot be expressed in terms of money.

The last of these three extracts could have been written about Wodehouse. His determination to reduce his taxes placed him in France at the outbreak of the second world war; the incompetence of his professional advisers led to unreasonable but highly public demands for underpayment of US taxes and ignorant charges of tax evasion. Without each of these circumstances, Cassandra would have had no catalyst for, and no reason to make, his broadcast in 1941, and England would certainly have benefited from the periodic presence of P G Wodehouse in the thirty years after the war.

By way of contrast, Bolton put in into operation one of Wodehouse's ideas for pulling the wool over the eyes of the authorities. In his book *Bolton and Wodehouse and Kern*[10], Lee Davis describes the incident as follows:

...[Guy] invented an alias for [his wife] Virginia — Stephen Powys — made it well known among various agents and managers that it was merely an alias for Virginia Bolton — and set up a separate tax account.

The purpose, one can reasonably assume, was principally to hide the receipt of royalties from the attention of the UK Revenue, but if the authorities saw through the ruse, to seek to argue that it was his wife's earnings, which may have been taxable at a lower rate than his own.

Stephen Powys was to be utilised as a pseudonym by Wodehouse himself in 1948 to disguise his involvement in the play *Don't Listen, Ladies*, which he wrote jointly with Guy Bolton for the London stage. It was perceived that any disadvantage which might otherwise arise from his unpopularity after the war could be neutralised, and the stratagem seems to have worked, as the play ran for 219 performances.

And for an interesting aside as to the general perception of income tax, Gerard Fairlie recalled in his autobiography *With Prejudice*[11] an edition of the radio programme *In Town Tonight* in which he appeared with Sapper, the creator of Bulldog Drummond, and the following conversation ensued:

Fairlie   ...Why did you think of me when you thought of Bulldog?

Sapper   Aren't you pleased?

Fairlie   We-ell, it has its drawbacks.

Sapper   Drawbacks? To be the original of a man at the mere mention of whose name criminals of two continents queue up to pay their income tax?

* * * * *

Having thoroughly surveyed the development of Wodehouse's experiences with the tax authorities in the US and the UK through the mid-1930's, it is now time to see how those experiences were translated into the written word for public consumption. Brief references can be found in two novels and one Mulliner story, a major element of the plot in another deals with the desire of an offstage character to evade (**NOT** avoid) customs duties, and **Right Ho, Jeeves**, the novel dedicated to Raymond Needham, has three references to which everybody can relate. A general diatribe against taxes appeared in the play **Who's Who** and during this period, **Louder and Funnier**[12], the collection of essays rewritten from **Vanity Fair**, was published, containing not only the expanded version of the essay **All About The Income Tax** (**Thoughts on the Income Tax**) but also an essay entitled **Round and About the Theatre**, in which he describes the position of a theatre audience which is seated, trapped, after having paid its money:

> What is at the root of the audience's unfortunate position is the old business of Taxation Without Representation. That is to say, the management of the theatre takes the audience's money but won't allow it a voice in the subsequent proceedings.

This essay is similar in tone to some of those referred to in chapter 3[13].

One other reference which has been traced comes from a somewhat obscure source, the published UK text of **Anything Goes**[14], which was not subject to rewriting to the same extent as the US version:

Reporter Mr Whitney, isn't it?

Whitney Yes

Reporter Will you step this way, Mr Whitney? We'd like to have a picture of you. *[Aside to another reporter.]* Elisha J. Whitney — you know, Wall Street — remember the income tax case .....

Chronologically, the first references in this period are found in **Hot Water**[15]; first during a conversation between Mr Gedge and his wife:

> "What", asked Mr Gedge, taking the chair vacated by the secretary, "is all this about your going to England? Medway tells me you're sailing on the afternoon boat."
>
> "I have had a letter from my lawyer in London. There has been some trouble about English Income Tax, and he says he must see me."

It could not have taken him too long to think up that part of the plot, written as it was just a few months after he had used the same words in real life.

And later in the book, Wodehouse felt it was necessary to summarise where all the principal characters were to be found:

> Mrs Gedge was in the office of her lawyer in London. His operations on her behalf in the matter of evasion of English Income Tax had dissatisfied her, and she was talking pretty straight to him.

In **Thank You, Jeeves**[16] the sole reference was familiar — a return to the consequence of years of heavy taxes on the ability of landowners to keep up their properties:

> Chuffy also owns the village of Chuffnell Regis — not that that does him much good, either. I mean to say, the taxes on the estate and all the expenses of repairs and whatnot come to pretty nearly as much as he gets out of the rents, making the whole thing more or less a washout.

In **Right Ho, Jeeves**[2], all three references concerned difficulties caused to Aunt Dahlia and indirectly to Bertie Wooster as a result of the aversion Uncle Tom Travers has to income tax and the demand for £ 58 1s 3d which he had just received. Aunt Dahlia introduces the subject while talking to Bertie:

"I'll tell you, Bertie. Up till now, when these subsidies were required, I have always been able to come to Tom in the gay, confident spirit of an only child touching an indulgent father for chocolate cream. But he's just had a demand from the income tax people for fifty-eight pounds, one and threepence, and all he's been talking about since I got back has been ruin and the sinister trend of socialistic legislation and what will become of us all."

I could readily believe it. This Tom has a peculiarity I've noticed in other very oofy men. Nick him for the paltriest sum, and he lets out a squawk you can hear at Land's End. He has the stuff in gobs, but he hates giving up.

The same cast is involved later:

"Is he still upset about that income tax money?"

"Upset is right. He says that Civilisation is in the melting-pot and that all thinking men can read the writing on the wall."

"What wall?"

"Old Testament, ass. Belshazzar's feast."

The effect on Tom's appearance of giving adequate thought to his tax problems, which presumably reflected those of Wodehouse himself in his more sombre moments, were described by Bertie on page 102, in the context of musing over the evening meal:

I was glad when it was over. What with having, on top of her other troubles, to rein herself back from the trough, Aunt Dahlia was a total loss as far as anything in the shape of brilliant badinage was concerned. The fact that he was fifty quid in the red and expecting

Civilisation to take a toss at any moment had caused Uncle Tom, who always looked a bit like a pterodactyl with a secret sorrow, to take on a deeper melancholy.

The Mulliner reference was very brief. Archibald Mulliner, visiting a pub in Bottleton East, realised that medicine for a bruised soul could be found there — in the rich smell of old liquors, and in the gay clamour of carefree men arguing about the weather, the Government, the Royal Family, greyhound racing, the tax on beer, pugilism, religion, and the price of bananas.[17]

In **Who's Who**, produced in 1934, (the dramatic equivalent of **If I Were You**[18]), Tony, the Earl of Droitwich, whose status was under threat, is engaged in conversation with the lovely Polly, former assistant to Syd Price in his hairdressing emporium:

Polly   I think you're wonderful, being so cheerful about it ... I know you must feel pretty awful really coming down from an earldom to this.

Tony   Don't you believe it. Being an earl nowadays is a mug's game. What with the inheritance tax, the land tax, the income tax, and all the rest of the little taxes, the terms "earl" and "deadbeat" are rapidly becoming synonymous.

One will never know what was the trigger behind that element of the plot of **The Luck of the Bodkins**[7] which consisted of the desire of Grayce, who does not actually appear, for her diamond necklace to be smuggled through the US Customs sheds in New York. It would be impractical to quote all the references, but the whole story is a splendid example of "non-series" Wodehouse (although a number of characters do reappear individually in other stories) and is commended to all readers.

There is, however, an additional brief reference to the feelings of one of the leading characters, Ivor Llewellyn, with which many readers may be expected to sympathise. (Bearing in mind the aftermath of Wodehouse's UK tax hearing, one can at least surmise that this is not autobiographical as far as UK tax inspectors are concerned.)

> It was at this point that Ivor Llewellyn had begun to behave like a Boy Scout. Nor can we fairly blame him. To each man is given his special fear. Some quail before income-tax assessors, others before traffic policemen. Ivor Llewellyn had always had a perfect horror of Customs inspectors.

That is all we can find in Wodehouse's writings from this traumatic period. But the successive experiences had made a deep impression, and even had there been no further battle with the tax authorities in the US one could look forward to much more comment in later texts! And it is with no little amusement that mentions of the dreaded topic, which was starting to dominate his life sufficiently to determine in which country he would live, would find their way into the lyrics of another close friend, Ira Gershwin.

For the 1936 *Ziegfeld Follies* he wrote two songs, the sentiments of which Wodehouse would have approved. In *Island in the West Indies* one stanza bears a passing resemblance to the feelings expressed in *Bongo on the Congo*:

> We'll lie around all day and just be lazy
> The world far behind
> (If that's not heaven then I'm crazy)
> With no taxes
> And with no axes to grind.

And a second song, *The Ballad of Baby Face McGinty*, whilst evidently based on the actions of one Al Capone, would also have struck a chord. It is too long to reproduce in full, but the last stanza and a half show how the authorities reacted to the success of Baby Face McGinty in holding up banks, dealing in booze and armaments, and indulging in arson, killing and rape, yet avoiding arrest (in part because he had ten gov'nors in his pay!):

"Get Baby Face McGinty!"
Said Mr Morgenthau
"He cheated on taxes, din't he?
That's one thing we can't allow!"
They got, they shot McGinty;
They never gave a damn
For you're up against true maniacs
When you don't pay up your income tax
The moral of McGinty
Is: Don't cheat your Uncle Sam.

So long, good-bye, McGinty —
On one thing you were lax
You could get away with murder
But not your income tax.

The following year, in the show *Shall We Dance*, Gershwin repeated the sentiment of the first of those two songs in *Slap That Bass*:

Zoom-zoom, zoom-zoom,
The world is in a mess
    With politics and taxes
    And people grinding axes,
There's no happiness.

After this phase, Ira Gershwin seems to have left the topic alone, at least until 1953, when a further two songs were produced — see chapter 8, page 215.

Footnotes

1 1977, Barrie & Jenkins
2 1934, Herbert Jenkins
3 1907, Cassell
4 and in book 9 of *Plum Stones — The Hidden P G Wodehouse* 1995, Galahad Books
5 and in **Lord Emsworth and Others** 1937, Herbert Jenkins

6   1990, Hutchinson
7   1935, Herbert Jenkins
8   1928, Methuen
9   1957, Peter Davies
10 1993, Heineman
11 1952, Hodder & Stoughton
12 1932, Faber & Faber
13 see eg, *Reviewing a Theatre Audience*, page 44
14 1936, Samuel French
15 1932, Herbert Jenkins
16 1934, Herbert Jenkins
17 1936, *Archibald and the Masses*, in **Young Men in Spats** 1936, Herbert Jenkins
18 1931, Herbert Jenkins

CHAPTER 6: 1937 to 1943 — LOST IN FRANCE

This period started well, with a minor triumph. On 28 December 1936, Wodehouse was able to write to Bill Townend and boast:

> I have a story coming out in **SEP** week ending Jan 30 which they think is the best I have ever done. It was sent to the **Red Book** during the time when my tax trouble was on and the **SEP** wouldn't buy my stuff, and they offered $ 2,000 for it, having given me $ 3,000 for my others. I refused this, and on landing in America rang up the editor and asked him to return my story — having called on Lorimer the previous day and, as I believe I told you, got him to agree that he would pay $ 4,000 for any stories of mine which he accepted. The editor of the **Red Book** raised the offer to $ 2,500; but I believed in the story so much that I turned it down, and am glad that I did, because the **Post** jumped at it. Title — **All's Well with Bingo**.

It can be assumed that Wodehouse enjoyed the freedom of a year in the US — which he spent in Hollywood on a one-year contract. He evidently decided to simplify his business structures, choosing in August 1937 to close SwissCo. He wrote to Reynolds in that month:

> The company SwissCo is being wound up; so all contracts and deals you handle for me from now on should be in my name ... don't forget you now knock off only 10% instead of the 15% which SwissCo was paying.

Simultaneously, he was conspiring with Leonora to provide some cash to meet a need being felt by her husband Peter Cazalet, and in a letter of 13 August, 1937, he demonstrated that the US tax case, indeed the question of income tax generally, had not ceased to be a topic of fascination and conversation in the Wodehouse household:

How clever of you to write me direct about that money. It would have spoiled Mummie's day. There is no need for her to know anything about it, as I have written to the Hongkong Bank to send old Pete a cheque, which you ought to get soon after this letter. What a damned nuisance these income tax people are. Have you noticed that there's always some sum like eighty pounds to be paid, however much you shell out.

It's much better recouping Pete on the quiet like this, as Mummie is so keen to get back to what we had before we paid out that twenty thousand to the American tax people. I shan't miss it from my Hongkong account, as it was all gambling winnings, anyway, so what the hell!

And even if he wanted to allow the subject to drop, the US government thought otherwise. The world's leading humorous writer was far too productive a source. So the very next month Wodehouse was writing to Townend:

This blasted administration has just knocked the bottom out of everything by altering the tax laws so that instead of paying a flat 10% as a non-resident alien I now have to pay ordinary citizen rate, which will take away about a third of what one earns.

The taxes are fantastic here — I mean in Hollywood. Because stars make so much over a short period before they go into the discard. Nelson Eddy, my neighbour, actually made $ 600,000 last year, and when all his taxes and expenses were paid found he had $ 50,000 left. Well, not bad, even so, one might say. But then the point is that in 1939 his income will perhaps be about tuppence.

The point is well taken, of course, and in the 1980s governments throughout the West finally saw the folly of ludicrously high tax rates. But one must also take comments like that with a pinch of salt — who knows how much of the $ 550,000 which Nelson Eddy spent went in "expenses" rather than tax!

It was around this time that Rafael Sabatini, another British subject, living in London, who earned money from the US whilst not resident there, was preparing to fight the IRS in the courts after having failed to convince them of the correctness of his views on the scope of US taxes on his various sources of income. This was a most important case, as it was a preliminary skirmish on the same battleground on which Wodehouse himself was to fight in the post-war years. It is therefore appropriate to review the facts and what the court said.

Sabatini was an author who was represented in the US by a firm of authors' representatives and part of the time by a New York bank. He never personally visited the US and appointed no-one as his taxation agent in the US. Some income was received for him by his representatives and reported for taxation, but that income was not the cause of the dispute with the authorities. Sabatini did not file tax returns for the years in dispute, claiming that he was not aware of his obligation to do so. The disputed tax arose from income from contracts for the publication or dramatisation of numerous books, and his authorisation of their use for motion pictures.

The Court confirmed that the payments from contracts for the right to publish his work in the US were clearly taxable in the US, even where, presumably because the works were already to be regarded as in the public domain, no formal copyright could exist. At the first level of hearing — before the Board of Tax Appeals — Sabatini had won on the question of the Motion Picture Rights. He granted world-wide rights to produce films based on five of his works, and the contract was made in England. The Board of Tax Appeals regarded this as a sale of property in England, and thus not taxable, on the face of it a highly rational decision.

The Court did not agree, preferring instead to regard it as a licence for use of the literary works in the US, and although the payment was received in the form of a lump-sum it was still taxable in the US as a royalty. The IRS also sought penalties for Sabatini's failure to file tax returns on time, arguing that he had no reasonable excuse for a failure to do so. The Court accepted that there was no evidence that any tax evasion whatsoever was intended. But it concluded, somewhat remarkably, that the taxpayer had shown no reasonable cause for failure to file tax returns, even though he believed he was liable for no taxes.

When reading chapter 7, that which deals with the increasingly arbitrary progress of Wodehouse's cases before the courts, it is as well to bear in mind the Sabatini case. In summary, what had happened was that in the 1930s, when international communication was much less common and straightforward than it is today, when it still took days to cross the Atlantic, *a person who never visited the US was penalised because he had shown no reasonable cause for neglecting an obligation* (of which he had probably never been told) *to file tax returns in a foreign country, and not reporting income which in any event the Board of Tax Appeals was to decide was not taxable*. Is that not an unduly high standard to expect, particularly in an unsophisticated era when computers did not exist, and competent tax advisers were few and far-between?

And before a cry goes up "But he didn't use any advisers, competent or otherwise", an ancillary point which arose in the Sabatini case related to a tax expert whom Sabatini did employ to represent him after the controversy blew up. This "expert" forged a letter to Sabatini to the effect that after careful consideration, the IRS had decided that no tax liability existed, and on the strength of this letter he collected his fee. He then employed an attorney to represent Sabatini in court who wrongly assumed that Sabatini would be present for the case before the Board of Tax Appeals. The expert, for some reason still in the picture, misled the attorney on certain facts, Sabatini was not present to assist, and the attorney was forced to concede the taxability of certain matters which otherwise he might have tried to fight.

That mishandling of the case may have caused an erroneous precedent to have been created, and that in turn may have had an influence on the result of the Wodehouse hearing in due course. So even if tax expertise had been used by Sabatini before the confrontation with the IRS, there is no saying that he would have been competently advised.

Before the Court hearing of the Sabatini case, on 4 November, 1937, Wodehouse arrived in Le Touquet, and stayed there, with occasional trips to England to stay with Leonora at Shipbourne Grange, Tonbridge, Kent, or to visit London. Short-term trips were allowed by UK tax authorities without causing residence to be imputed, provided they were carefully limited, and Wodehouse appears on the evidence to have kept to the rules.

Like Sabatini, Wodehouse was to come before the tax courts. One of the matters which he was to dispute was the treatment of income from the sale of various rights to SwissCo. As has been shown, his attorneys decided in the long run that this was a liability rather than a benefit, and some correspondence has survived concerning the closure of that company a few months before the termination of its contract with Wodehouse. Unfortunately, the material available does not explain exactly how the closure was carried out.

On 31 December, 1937, SwissCo wrote to inform Reynolds that it had been decided to close the company, as a result of which SwissCo had transferred back to Wodehouse all his copyrights. Wodehouse himself notified Reynolds formally on 12 January, 1938, saying the decision was made following a meeting of lawyers, accountants, etc, and that the winding-up was likely to take a year. In this letter he notified Reynolds that all future payments should be made "to me personally. I think you had better send drafts to this address — if there are any drafts!"

Wodehouse's next ploy was to seek to benefit from a policy of legally splitting his income with Ethel. By now he had learned the need to follow correct procedures — in the subsequent court case the Judge commented that there was a "meticulous adherence to form" in that notices were sent to the taxpayer's agent and remittances and reports were made as though the stories were jointly owned. In the 12 January letter he said:

> Will you get in touch with Watson Washburn and have him explain the arrangements about the money. He sent me a deed of gift to sign, by which I transfer half my interest in the story to my wife. I imagine the best plan, when the time for making the payment arrives, will be for you to send two drafts, one to me and one to Ethel Wodehouse.

Ethel herself wrote a few days later — on 8 February — to reaffirm this:

> I talked to Plum on the telephone, and he asked me to write to you and tell you that he would like all future payments on all his works to be divided equally between us, half to be paid to Plum, and half to myself.

This became a consistent procedure — as illustrated on 3 June, 1939, in another letter from PGW to Reynolds:

> So glad the short stories are selling. I had a letter from Washburn saying I'd have to pay $ 2,800 extra income tax over and above the 10% you deduct, so will you give him that out of the check for **Scratch Man** and send the rest and the money for **Bramley** to Ethel Wodehouse and P G Wodehouse in separate checks.

There is no doubt at all that it was the fallout from the UK tax case and the double taxation of US earnings which would be created by existing UK tax laws if he moved to the UK — possibly influenced by the level of US taxes if he lived permanently in the US — that caused both the Wodehouses to be in Le Touquet when war broke out. They were reluctant to leave the town when discretion might have suggested urgent action, primarily because of the quarantine regulations which would have prevented their dogs travelling with them. According to Lee Davis, Guy Bolton said:

> It was the damned dogs. Neither one of them wanted to leave them, and that was the reason they were captured.

Although it is not necessary to go once again over all the ground of the unfortunate wartime phase of Wodehouse's career, it may be of interest to readers to provide contemporary comments about the catalyst for Cassandra's broadcast, and an insight into why Duff Cooper, an extremely insecure and egotistical politician, permitted the broadcast which has been so roundly condemned for the last 45 years.

Wodehouse's occasional friend Charles Graves was one of six persons lunching with Duff Cooper on 4 July, 1941, as part of the latter's attempt, in his role as Minister of Propaganda, to get to know British journalists better. He described the lunch in the following terms in his book *Off the Record*[1]:

> Lunched with Duff Cooper in a private room at the Savoy. It was a curious party — six professional individualists: Cassandra, whose real name is Connor, of the *Mirror,* spectacled, with blue lidless eyes and an unidentifiable accent; plump Francis Williams, who was bracketed with me by Lord Haw-Haw as the two most dangerous men in Fleet Street; wild-haired Michael Foot, spectacled and very keen-looking; A J Cummings, in a pale suit, a sly Liberal; Hannen Swaffer, who arrived late, talked loudly, then subsided and ostentatiously read the *Evening Standard* through most of the meal. Conversation was mostly about propaganda. Cassandra asked why Duff Cooper didn't resign. The reply was that it would be regarded as a great triumph for the Germans if he did. Personally, I am dubious. He said that it would be fundamentally unsound if Walter Monckton or he walked out.

126

I raised the subject of P G Wodehouse, and said that Ronald Squire or Cecil Parker should be put up to a reply, speaking as Jeeves about their poor Master. Duff Cooper said that nobody could imitate Wodehouse. I said this was unnecessary. We could take complete sentences of real Wodehouse out of his various novels and make them fit the case. Cassandra then offered to broadcast to America himself, knocking Wodehouse for his tax evasion. I regard this as silly, but Duff Cooper jumped at it. Michael Foot was mostly interested in getting America into the war by better propaganda, and, like all the others, he used his hands to argue. Duff Cooper replied that Gerald Campbell was on his way back today and he himself would be glad to add a nought to any sum of money that Campbell thought necessary for propaganda in the US. Nobody, however, was allowed to finish a sentence throughout the meal, which was preceded by some vicious yellow vodka.

Another of those attending, Francis Williams, recalled the same lunch in his autobiography **Nothing So Strange**[2]:

[Duff Cooper] asked me to introduce him to editors and columnists at a series of lunches. These lunches tended to go on a long time and to give everyone present the impression that he had not much to do. One of them had an eccentric result. A good deal of brandy and vodka had been taken — the vodka to toast the Russians who were now our allies — and William Connor, Cassandra of the *Daily Mirror*, began to complain rather truculently that much more attention was paid to American journalists by the Government than British. He cited Quentin Reynolds, whose gifts as a raconteur had much endeared him to the Prime Minister and who had been given time on the BBC to deliver a rip-roaring attack on Hitler, whom he addressed by his original name of Schickelgruber. He himself, said Cassandra, could have given a much better broadcast if given the chance, but they daren't let him on the air for fear that he might attack some of their pets.

Duff Cooper, who by now had consumed a good deal of brandy, denied having any pets and was thereupon attacked by Cassandra for doing nothing about P G Wodehouse, who had fallen into German hands when France was invaded and had made a couple of silly broadcasts about life in captivity which indicated a juvenile remoteness from real life and from the current mood of the British people rather than anything more serious. The argument ended with Duff Cooper inviting Cassandra to broadcast on Wodehouse or to Wodehouse if he preferred to do it that way, with the promise that he could say whatever he liked.

Later that afternoon the script was produced. The BBC refused to put it on air. They considered it vulgar, extravagant and probably libellous. Conscious of his lunchtime undertaking and of what Cassandra would say if he failed to live up to it Duff Cooper insisted. Thereupon the BBC demanded written orders under the wartime regulation which suspended the BBC's independent constitution and made it subject to the direction of the Minister of Information. They wanted evidence that they had acted under duress if a libel writ arrived after the war. The written order was sent, the only one issued, I think, throughout the war, and was locked up by the BBC in its vaults for safe-keeping. Duff Cooper regretted the broadcast as soon as it was made, and so, later, did Cassandra himself.

The last surviving member of this luncheon party, Michael Foot, recently commented in a letter to the present writer:

Since the reports were taken down at the time it is certainly difficult to dispute any item in them. But I certainly do not think there was any discussion of Wodehouse's alleged tax evasion.

So a picture emerges of an incompetent government minister, a few days before getting the sack, subrogating his authority whilst under the influence of alcohol to a taunting journalist attacking him in private. With his judgment, such as it was, impaired by drink, he sought to recover his reputation at the expense of a defenceless individual who would have no right of reply. And later, when the spiritual haze had lightened, he did not dare renege on his promise to Cassandra, despite realising the error of his ways.

In the circumstances, this writer finds another quotation from Charles Graves, this time from *The Bad Old Days*[3], most appropriate:

> ... the Duchess of Sutherland's fancy dress ball the following week was a great success. The Prince of Wales appeared in a beard. Mr Churchill went as a barrister in a wig, Lord Louis Mountbatten was a black rooster, Mr Duff Cooper appeared as a rat, scampering over the floor as well as his figure permitted. But the guest who fascinated me most was Lord Portarlington as a seventeenth-century dowager.

... but does not understand why Graves thought Duff Cooper was in fancy dress.

The broadcast by Cassandra was actually in two forms, one for domestic consumption, and a considerably longer version for the US public which included the sentence:

A smart guy who, when the Internal Revenue Department called round for a slight item of $ 125,000 of income tax owing, found that the fun-doctor had flown.

In the furore which followed the broadcasts, ignorant members of the public in the UK also sought to bring Wodehouse's tax difficulties into the debate. These are generally to be found in the correspondence in the *Daily Telegraph* columns after the Berlin broadcasts, most of which are quoted in Iain Sproat's book *Wodehouse at War*[4]:

From W A Darlington   July 2, 1941

Throughout life he has taken the easy and comfortable way. The beginning of the last war found him in America. He remained there, and amassed a comfortable fortune, while his friends fought. He was equally easy-going in his money affairs, for he came into the public eye later when the United States authorities demanded £ 50,000 of unpaid income tax from him.

From A A Milne   July 3, 1941

This, I felt, had always been Wodehouse's attitude to life. He has encouraged in himself a natural lack of interest in "politics" — "politics" being all the things which the grown-ups talk about at dinner when one is hiding under the table. Things, for instance, like the last war, which found and kept him in America; and post-war taxes, which chased him backwards and forwards across the Atlantic until he finally found sanctuary in France.

From Sax Rohmer   July 7, 1941

See chapter 2, page 21

[Sax Rohmer himself, advised like Wodehouse by Watson Washburn of Perkins, Malone and Washburn, fought his corner against the IRS through to the Court of Appeals in 1946, but lost on all counts. See chapter 7 for more detail.]

From Bill Townend   July 9, 1941

That he had trouble over his income-tax has often been brought up against him. As Mr W A Darlington says, the US Government demanded £ 50,000 of unpaid income-tax from him. What Mr Darlington omits to say is that the US Government after prolonged negotiation accepted one-seventh the sum originally asked for. Had the larger amount been proven legally theirs, they would not have accepted the smaller.

It was not only the correspondents of the **Daily Telegraph** who distorted the facts in respect of his US tax dispute in connection with a personal view of the Berlin Broadcasts. Harold Nicolson, the husband of Vita Sackville-West, was a writer, a part-time socialist politician, a Governor of the BBC from 1941 to 1946, and a Junior Minister at the Ministry of Information from 1940 to 1941, until he was removed from that post by Churchill — along with Duff Cooper, the Minister himself — one week after the infamous Cassandra broadcast. In his diary for 4 January 1944, he wrote[5]:

I get a letter today from John Masefield, as President of the Incorporated Society of Authors etc. asking me why the BBC have "banned" P G Wodehouse. If anybody we do not want to employ is regarded as "banned" then the BBC will lose all freedom of selection. Moreover, there is no doubt [?] that Wodehouse allowed himself, for a "consideration", to be used for broadcasts which were in the interest of the enemy. As such he is a traitor and should not be used. I do not want to see Wodehouse shot on Tower Hill. But I resent the theory that "poor P.G. is so innocent that he is not responsible." A man who has shown such ingenuity and resource in evading British and American income tax cannot be classified as unpractical.

One is not surprised to read opinions like this — they represent the fairly standard expressions of envy accorded to a master of the writer's profession, who was so much more successful both professionally and financially than the writer himself. A master, moreover, who had never seen the need to join the dilettante group of which Nicolson — and more especially his wife — were a part.

Neither should one be surprised at the sheer hypocrisy of the last sentence, concerning the "evasion of British and American taxes", when it is compared to an entry in his diary for 6 March, 1932: that, in relation to a journey his wife is proposing

> ...we CANNOT AFFORD IT — WE ARE POOR PEOPLE THESE DAYS — *[capitals as per original]*....We work out that our life costs us no less than £ 240 a month. That at present we have £ 600 and about £ 1,000 owing from America. <u>We do not want to use the latter because of income tax.</u>

This entry hardly suggests that Nicolson was unaware of the benefits to be obtained by planning one's affairs to avoid or defer the incidence of taxation!

It may be appropriate to include here the very helpful comments by Iain Sproat on the charges of tax evasion made by correspondents to the press:

In Malcolm Muggeridge's essay on the Wodehouse affair, published in the volume entitled *Tread Softly For You Tread On My Jokes*[6], Muggeridge describes how he visited Duff Cooper in Paris in 1944, where Cooper was then British Ambassador. According to Muggeridge, Cooper said to him that Wodehouse "had always evaded reality and his responsibilities as a citizen". This charge of the evasion of responsibilities appears to refer to Cooper's belief, and to the belief of others already quoted, that Wodehouse had managed to evade fighting in the First World War, and that he owed the U.S. Inland Revenue Service substantial amounts of unpaid income tax, and had contrived to pay as little British tax as possible for many years. ...

As far as Duff Cooper's, and others' comments about "irresponsibility" over tax matters are concerned, the implications of these comments are, in one instance, somewhat unfair, and in another, wholly false. It was, in fact, Ethel Wodehouse who insisted on their travels to avoid, perfectly legally, paying more tax than was necessary to both British and American authorities. Ethel liked having plenty of money — not least to pay for her gambling. Nonetheless, Wodehouse must bear responsibility in that he acquiesced.

Regarding the charge, referred to implicitly by Duff Cooper and others, that he illegally evaded United States income tax — the U.S. authorities in 1934 were demanding some $ 50,000 from him — this charge was false. The facts were set out by Wodehouse's fellow author Sax Rohmer in the letter to the *Daily Telegraph* of July 1941, already quoted. In the end this particular tax demand was settled amicably, as Wodehouse's friend, Bill Townend, pointed out in his letter to the *Daily Telegraph*, with the U.S. authorities accepting only one-seventh of what they had originally demanded from Wodehouse.

The weekly magazine *Picture Post* jumped on the bandwagon, and introducing an article about the wartime broadcasts on 19 July, 1941, the magazine says:

> ... It is true that he has never shown an interest in politics — he was in America when the last war broke out, then an up-and-coming author of 34. He stayed there until the allies won. Then, when America wanted a large amount of income tax, he resorted to France, where he settled down comfortably in a charming villa.

In the US the press were to some degree lower in profile, doing what they could to help obtain Wodehouse's release — and, ironically, indirectly contributing to his problems, as it was his desire to thank all his supportive correspondents that had originally led him to make the broadcasts to, as he thought, the neutral American listener.

For example, the *Saturday Evening Post* readers asked all sorts of questions, including — did he have to pay tax in Germany on his articles sent to the United States? Reynolds tried to reply to the letters that were passed to him. In response to an enquiry from J E Walkin of Lewiston, NY, he replied on 26 November, 1941:

> I am sure Mr Wodehouse would be glad to have me tell you that approximately half of [his earnings] will be paid to the US government in income tax.

He followed this up by responding to Mr H L Day of Minneapolis, who had enquired on 18 December whether the German Government receives through taxation or in any manner any part of the money the *SEP* was paying for the then current serial, in the following terms:

> This money is being held in New York pending the cessation of the war and Mr Wodehouse's freedom ... A large part of this money is paid by us on behalf of Mr Wodehouse to the US Government for his income taxes.

134

Reynolds had generally been keeping an eye on his client's interests, to the limited extent possible whilst Wodehouse was in Germany. In January 1941, for example, he wrote to Malcolm Johnson of Doubleday Doran & Co:

> PGW owned SwissCo, wound up, final taxes owed by the corporation have now been arrived at and agreed by the government and that amount is $ 755.63. It is desirable to have these taxes paid... Interest will run on this amount, probably penalties; also we think it is very desirable that there shouldn't be unpaid taxes which Wodehouse owes the government.
>
> ... [paragraph in which he asks Doubleday Doran to pay the tax and charge Wodehouse's account].
>
> Wodehouse, having gotten into tax difficulties a few years ago, expressed himself as very desirous of having all taxes paid and there is no question in the minds of our lawyers that this amount has to be paid. As far as I can foresee the future, I think Wodehouse would be grateful if you did this rather than the reverse.

In **Performing Flea**, the book of letters written by Wodehouse to Bill Townend published in the UK in 1953, many of the letters included were modified to improve what today would be known as "reader-friendliness". The words from the original letters have been used in this book wherever possible, but not all the originals could be traced.

One such laments the approach of journalists, for whom the apparent quality of a story, a headline, or a telling phrase is more important than the professionalism of trust and honesty. The reader will be familiar with the furore caused by the reporter from the *Los Angeles Times* who published an off-the-record conversation as an interview on the state of Hollywood in May 1931. In a letter stated to be dated 18 April, 1953, Wodehouse was reminiscing about the post-internment period, and

135

commenting on this very disability which seems to afflict almost all known journalists, at least those from the "popular" or "tabloid" press:

> ... writers on daily and weekly papers always will go all out for the picturesque. When they interview you, they invariably alter and embroider.
>
> As a rule, this does not matter much. If on your arrival in New York you are asked "What do you think of our high buildings?" and you reply, "I think your high buildings are wonderful", and it comes out as "I think your high buildings are wonderful. I should like to see some of these income-tax guys jump off the top of them", no harm is done. The sentiment pleases the general public, and even the officials of the Internal Revenue Department probably smile indulgently, as men who know they are going to have the last laugh. But when there is a war in progress, it is kinder to the interviewee not to indulge the imagination.

Generally, the period of internment and the years to 1942 were relatively quiet as far as actual — rather than perceived or brewing — tax problems were concerned. But 1943 brought the first indications that the Wodehouse tax difficulties were about to flare up again — although he was not to be informed until 1944.

During 1943, the Alien Property Custodian in Washington sent a series of forms to Paul Reynolds to obtain information about Wodehouse's earnings from the musical comedies. In his reply (15 April, 1943) Reynolds protested vigorously:

> Representatives of various branches of the Treasury Department have been in here a considerable number of times; twice they have copied verbatim the entire Wodehouse ledger account. I mention this because we have nothing to hide from the government but have reported the situation to the government not once but over and over again.

On 15 June, 1943, Reynolds received yet another notice of lien (see page 138) in relation to Wodehouse's tax liabilities — this time $ 21,328.82 plus interest and penalties of $ 17,382.99 regarding alleged underpayments in 1937, a year for which an audit had already been carried out and a tax repayment made! This was accompanied by a demand, called a "Notice of levy" (see page 139), which was not to be taken lightly, and Reynolds immediately paid over the $ 23,624.48 he had in his possession.

Reynolds decided to send the press an official notice about the tax department intrigues (23 June, 1943). He also wrote to Senator Walter F George and to Henry Morgenthau Jnr (remember Baby Face McGinty, p117?) on 24 June in the following terms:

Under the compulsion of the notice of levy served on us by a representative of the Treasury Department on June 16, 1943 for alleged unpaid income tax of P G Wodehouse in the amount of $ 38,711.81 for the year 1937, we have sent to the Collector of Internal Revenue our check for $ 23,624.48, representing the entire amount now owing by us to Mr Wodehouse. As Mr Wodehouse's literary agents in the United States for more than twenty years, we protest against this levy and the manner in which the Treasury Department has proceeded against Mr Wodehouse in this regard.

Mr Wodehouse's 1937 Federal income tax return was filed June 3, 1938. The 1937 Federal income tax return of SwissCo, SA, a Swiss corporation to which Mr Wodehouse had assigned certain of his copyrights, was filed May 28, 1938. A tax of $ 4,526.40 was paid on Mr Wodehouse's account, and a tax of $ 8,514.12 was paid on SwissCo's account, on or before those two dates. Subsequently, in December, 1940, after examinations by at least two different income tax auditors, the Treasury Department ruled that Mr Wodehouse had paid $ 723.89 too much, and refunded this amount to him. At the same time, the Treasury

NOTICE OF TAX LIEN UNDER INTERNAL REVENUE LAWS

Form 668—Revised May 1939
TREASURY DEPARTMENT
INTERNAL REVENUE SERVICE

No. 2030

UNITED STATES INTERNAL REVENUE,

3rd DISTRICT OF .... New York

June 15 ...., 19 43.

Pursuant to the provisions of Sections 3670, 3671, and 3672 of the Internal Revenue Code of the United States, notice is hereby given that there have been assessed under the Internal Revenue laws of the United States against the following-named taxpayer, taxes (including interest and penalties) which after demand for payment thereof remain unpaid, and that by virtue of the above-mentioned statutes the amount of said taxes, together with penalties, interest, and costs that may accrue in addition thereto, is a lien in favor of the United States upon all property and rights to property belonging to said taxpayer, to wit:

Name of taxpayer .... Pelham G. Wodehouse

Residence or place of business .... c/o Perkins, Malone & Washburn 58 West 44th St. NYC

Nature of tax .... Income

Taxable period .... 1937 ...., 19

Amount of tax assessed .... $ 21,328.62

Additional (penalty) tax assessed and interest .... $ 17,382.99
$ 58,711.61

Date assessment list received ...., 19

Collector.

CERTIFICATE OF OFFICER AUTHORIZED BY LAW TO TAKE ACKNOWLEDGMENTS

STATE OF .... New York
COUNTY OF .... New York } ss:

On this day personally appeared before me a .... Notary Public
in and for the State and County aforesaid, ... Joseph T. Higgins (Official title)
Collector of Internal Revenue for the .... Third .... district of .... New York
to me well known as the person who executed the foregoing instrument, and acknowledged that he executed the same for the purposes therein expressed.

In witness whereof I have hereunto set my hand and official seal, this the 15th
day of .... June ...., 19 43.

[SEAL]

Alfred Simon

NOTARY PUBLIC, New York County
N. Y. Co. Clk's No. 40, Reg. No. 48 902
Commission expires March 30, 1944

TO .... George J. H. Follmer
Clerk of the United States Courthouse
for the Southern District of New York
United States Courthouse
Foley Square, New York.

2—10364

138

Form 668-A
TREASURY DEPARTMENT
INTERNAL REVENUE SERVICE
Revised Nov. 1933

NOTICE OF LEVY

UNITED STATES OF AMERICA,

........**Third**..... Collection District,

State of ...**New York**_____

To ___**Paul R. Reynolds & Son**_____
    (Name of person holding property, moneys, etc., belonging to taxpayer)

At ___**599 Fifth Avenue, New York City**_____ ,

You are hereby notified that there is now due, owing, and unpaid from ..**Pelham G. Wodehouse**.

__**c/o Perkins, Malone & Washburn**_____ to the United States of America the sum of
    36 West 44th Street, NYC (Address of taxpayer)

__**Thirty-Eight Thousand Seven Hundred Eleven Dollars**_____ dollars ($__**38,711.81**____)
    (Insert amount of tax, penalties, and interest due) **and Eighty-One Cents**
as and for an internal revenue tax.

You are further notified that all property, rights to property, moneys, credits, and/or bank deposits

now in your possession and belonging to the aforesaid ..**Pelham G. Wodehouse**_____ ,
    (Insert name of taxpayer)

and all sums of money owing from you to the said _____**Pelham G. Wodehouse**_____
    (Insert name of taxpayer)

are hereby seized and levied upon for the payment of the aforesaid tax, together with penalties and in-

terest, and demand is hereby made upon you for the sum of ..**Thirty-Eight Thousand Seven Hundred**
    Eleven Dollars and Eighty-One Cents
    (Insert amount of tax, penalties, and interest)

dollars ($__**38,711.81**_____.) of the amount now owing from you to the said

__**Pelham G. Wodehouse**_____ or for such lesser sum as you may be indebted to
    (Insert name of taxpayer)

him, to be applied in payment of the said tax liability.

Dated at __**110 East 45th Street, NYC**____

this __**15th**____ day of __**June**_____, 19**45.**

_____
    Collector of Internal Revenue.

U. S. GOVERNMENT PRINTING OFFICE   2—12503

Notice of lien (facing) and notice of levy concerning
income tax, penalty and interest alleged to be due.

139

Department ruled that SwissCo had paid $ 395.90 too much, and issued a check in refund of this overpayment.

Prior to these refunds, I am informed that the Treasury Department made a full and elaborate investigation of Mr Wodehouse's and SwissCo's tax liability.

Normally, the Treasury Department is prohibited by law from attempting to collect additional taxes more than three years after the due dates of the income tax returns, which in this case would have been June 15, 1941. Nevertheless, the Treasury Department has in the last year again audited Mr Wodehouse's 1937 returns, and as I am advised by Mr Wodehouse's attorney, have gone so far as to demand inspection of his correspondence with Mr Wodehouse, despite the fact that for many centuries the confidential nature of communications between attorney and client has been as much respected by the law as the confessional.

Notwithstanding these repeated and exhaustive investigations over a period of five years, after what was intended to be a final settlement two and a half years ago, involving great loss of time to both Treasury employees and Mr Wodehouse's representatives in this country, it appears that the Treasury was still unable to make up its mind as to Mr Wodehouse's 1937 tax liability, for his attorney informs me he was asked on June 14, 1943 (for the first time) to sign a waiver of the statute of limitations, which under ordinary circumstances would have finally run two years before. When he declined, the Treasury made a "jeopardy" assessment on June 15, 1943, instead of adopting the usual procedure of mailing a letter of proposed deficiency, permitting the question of liability to be determined by the Board of Tax Appeals in an orderly way, and any additional tax found due to be collected thereafter.

The intent of Congress in authorizing the drastic remedy of jeopardy assessment was to limit its use to cases in which the Commissioner of Internal Revenue believed that the collection of the proposed deficiency would be jeopardized by delay in seizing the taxpayer's property. Such belief in this case is difficult to justify, since the Treasury Department has known for three years that all Mr Wodehouse's property in the United States has been frozen under its control. The jeopardy assessment was followed by the filing of a lien with the District Court here, which gave rise to publicity, with the unfavourable implication that Mr Wodehouse was delinquent in meeting his taxes, without giving him or his representative a chance to be heard in his defense.

Mr Wodehouse is a British subject who has with his wife been a prisoner of the Germans for more than three years. But if this method of arbitrary seizure of property can be practiced against him, two and a half years after his tax liability has been fully audited and settled, it can equally well be used against any American citizen at any time. This is susceptible of such ruinous abuse in the hands of overzealous administrators that we respectfully suggest that the Revenue Act be amended to provide specifically that no jeopardy assessment be made except by order of a District Judge of the United States, upon application by the Commissioner of Internal Revenue, which shall satisfy the Judge that the taxpayer is about to leave the country or transfer or conceal his assets.

The letter to Senator George was duly sent on to Colin F Stam, head of the Alien Property department, and, by post on 12 July, Reynolds received a very formal, bureaucratic response that the departments concerned had acted in compliance with the current law.

Paul Revere Reynolds was in touch with Leonora, keeping her in touch with the progress of events, and she wrote a warmly appreciative reply, full of common-sense, on 17 August, 1943:

> How sickening about the jeopardy tax — perhaps in time it will end happily tho I suppose there is absolutely nothing to be done at present except see that all taxes etc are paid bang on time etc which you obviously do. I feel very helpless but I know that you will tell me if there is anything that I can do. I should however like Peter [*Cazalet, her husband*] to know the exact position. Would you ask Mr Washburn if he'd be kind enough to write me an exact resumé of the whole position and his opinion of it all. I shouldn't try to digest it myself but would like an accountant here to explain it to me so he needn't keep to words of one syllable for my benefit!

In relation to this jeopardy assessment and the payment made, Reynolds Jnr. was not able to communicate directly with Wodehouse until 8 September, 1944, when he reported on what had happened:

> Your London solicitors, who were informed, will have told you that the American Government has seized all your money that was in our possession. They took it by law and by force. Mr Washburn thinks it will ultimately be recovered.

As indicated above, readers should be under no illusion that Wodehouse was the only author to be investigated or asked for more tax. Apart from Sabatini and Sax Rohmer, many documented examples can be found, and it is appropriate to include here a further extract from Paul R Reynolds 1972 book *The Middle Man*[7]:

> The war produced changes in the law which in individual cases could work hardship or even hurt morale. With one author I was involved in a

142

controversy with the bureaucracy of the Internal Revenue Service. I do not know whether I was right or not. Lewis Ritchie, a captain in the British Navy, had written before the war some quite distinguished short naval sea stories under the pen name of Barthemeus. With the United States in the war, naval stories became popular. In the spring of 1942 Little, Brown & Company agreed to publish a collection of these stories, paying $ 2,500 against hoped-for royalties. At this time we were required by law to withhold 10 percent of the income of a nonresident alien and pay such amount to the United States Internal Revenue Service for American income tax. I duly paid the Government $ 250 and forewarded the balance to Ritchie's bank in London. In the summer of 1942 the 10 per cent withholding tax was increased by Congress to 40 percent and made retroactive to January first of that year. I received a paper addressed to Ritchie dunning him for $ 750 (10 percent of $ 2,500 or $ 250 had been paid the Government; now 30 percent more or $ 750 was due). Ritchie was at this time commanding a battleship in the Mediterranean. I felt that he had enough to worry about fighting the war and should not be inflicted with this news about American taxes. I replied to a number in the Internal Revenue (men do not write letters in that bureaucracy, numbers send printed forms) and said that Captain Ritchie was in the British Navy, that had he been in our Navy he would not have been asked to pay income tax at this time, that Ritchie could not possibly pay now because English citizens were not allowed to buy dollars. There was no reply.

A year later a further form came from the government. Ritchie was charged $ 750 plus interest plus penalties. I composed a fiery letter to the Internal Revenue number; I thought my letter was a beauty. No reply. Each year up to 1952 a printed form demanding payment arrived from the Internal Revenue Bureau, the amount increasing annually because of mounting interest and penalties. Each year upon receiving the tax demand form I sent to the number a copy of my original fiery letter. At no time was my correspondence acknowledged.

In London in 1950 I met Ritchie, now Sir Lewis Ritchie. He had been knighted for his war services but no money comes with a knighthood. Living in a cottage outside of London he was taking care of his wife, who was bedridden with arthritis. His income was the meager retirement pay granted a British naval officer. Ritchie was not wealthy. I did not tell him of the United States Government's claim against him for income taxes.

In 1952 an Internal Revenue agent telephoned me. He wanted Captain Ritchie's address. I told the agent I would not give him the address unless forced to by a court of law. I did not tell the agent of my fear that if Ritchie knew of the income tax demand, he might try to pay it. The agent said that he had on file nine identical letters from me. I said that I hoped that he had read at least one of them. The agent said that if I would write the Bureau a letter stating that Captain Ritchie was indigent and could not pay, they would drop the matter and close the file. I refused to do that but I said, "Why don't you write me such a letter?" A few days later I received a letter (not a form with a number) stating that because Captain Ritchie was destitute and unable to pay they were dropping any further action to collect the income tax and were closing out the file. I promptly threw the letter in the wastepaper basket. Somewhat later Sir Lewis Ritchie died. He was never aware of the American Government's income tax demands. I am proud of having won this battle with the Internal Revenue.

And so say all of us.

The scene was now set for the even greater traumas which the tax man was to create, and which would finally influence Wodehouse's writings and correspondence to a considerably greater degree than heretofore.

* * * * *

One can find indications in Wodehouse's work even during this period, in which only a limited amount of new material was published, that he was feeling sore with the tax authorities.

In the story **Buried Treasure**[8], which concerns the income potential of "Joyeuse", the luxurious moustache adorning the face of Lord Bromborough, Brancepeth Mulliner is talking to Bromborough's butler, Phipps:

> If Lord Bromborough's face in its stark fundamentals is as you describe it, I can guarantee that in less than no time I shall be bounding about the place trying to evade super-tax.

In **Summer Moonshine**[9], he first briefly commented on the income expectations of a plasterer (one who, on behalf of creditors, serves writs on reluctant debtors) in the following terms:

> If, in these last twenty-five years, Toots's brother Sam had raised himself from the modest position of a singing waiter to that of America's foremost process server, the fact did him credit, of course, and showed what could be accomplished by a man of grit and enterprise, but it was no longer possible to entertain any illusion that he might have the stuff in any appreciable quantity. Even the most gifted of plasterers does not pay super-tax.

And then he provided some dialogue which came right up from the bootstraps, gathering every drop of emotion that he could muster. Princess Dwornitzchek, the first speaker, is talking to Joe Vanringham:

145

"Are you going back [to the hall] now? If so, I can give you a lift."

"Thanks."

"Unless you have any more street fighting to do?"

"No, I'm through for the day. I hear you have been revisiting New York."

"Yes. I returned the day before yesterday. I had to go over and see my lawyer about my income tax. The Treasury people were making the most absurd claims."

"Soaking the rich?"

"Trying to soak the rich."

"I hope they skinned you to the bone."

"No. As a matter of fact, I came out of it very well. Have you a cigarette?"

"Here you are."

"Thank you. Yes, I won out all along the line."

And in a mood of wishful thinking, perhaps, he gave special attributes including confident determination to Princess Dwornitzchek:

"[Joe] watched her as she sat there smoking and smiling quietly at some thought that seemed to be amusing her, and tried to analyse the murderous feelings which she had always aroused in him. She was, as he had said, undefeatable, and he came to the conclusion that it was this impregnability of hers that caused them. She had no heart and a vast amount of money, and this enabled her to face the world encased in triple brass. He had in her presence a sense of futility, as if he were a very small wave beating up against a large complacent cliff. No doubt the officials of the United States Treasury Department had felt the same.

In **Quick Service**[10], Wodehouse made a muted protest about the level of taxes in the US, shortly after he had suffered from the increased tax rate from 10% to 33%. Miss Pym, the first speaker, is conversing with the American millionaire J B Duff:

"Who's [Hetty Green]?"

"She was one of the richest women in America."

"I suppose everybody makes tons of money there?"

"Yes, and when they've made it, what happens? Does Mister Whiskers let 'em keep it? Not a hope. Listen," said Mr Duff, beginning to swell, "lemme — "

He paused. He had been about to speak freely and forcefully of some of the defects of the existing Administration in his native country, but he felt that a *tête-à-tête* with a charming woman was not the occasion for it. Better to wait till he was back with the boys at the Union League Club.

"Plenty taxes in America these days," he said, condensing the gist of it into a sentence.

Footnotes

1 Hutchinson. Publication date uncertain — early 1940's
2 1970, Cassell
3 1951, Faber and Faber
4 1981, Milner

5 *Harold Nicolson Diaries* 1980, Collins
6 1966, Collins
7 1972, William Morrow (NY)
8 **Lord Emsworth & Others** 1937, Herbert Jenkins
9 1938, Herbert Jenkins
10 1940, Herbert Jenkins

CHAPTER 7: 1944 to 1950 — THE COMEDY OF ERRORS

It must have come as rather a shock, when the Wodehouses were recovering from the trauma of the war, internment and the after-effects of the broadcasts controversy, to hear that, not satisfied with their actions in respect of 1937, the Treasury Department had decided to go over all their previous tax declarations, (ie 1921 to 1943), especially Ethel Wodehouse's accounts for the work which had appeared during the war.

Just to add a little variety into their work, and make sure their agents were not bored by the repetitive nature of their activities, the Internal Revenue Service extended its line of investigation into possible gift tax liabilities arising from the assignment to Ethel of a half-interest in PGW's work. Once again, it should be made clear that Wodehouse was not being singled out for investigation — the letter asking for information from Reynolds' office referred to Rose Elizabeth Rohmer as well as Ethel Wodehouse. The relevant text of the request, dated 27 October, 1944, is as follows:

> This office has under consideration the possible gift tax liability of [*Pelham G Wodehouse and Sax Rohmer*], for whom, it is our understanding, you act as agent in the collection of royalties and payments made in the United States, arising out of the use of the literary works of these persons.
>
> For the proper disposition of this question, it is necessary that this office be furnished with a statement showing:
>
> a) The amounts paid to Ethel Wodehouse and the dates of payment thereof from 1938 down to date, from any source based on the use for any purpose of the works of Mr Wodehouse, entitled

"**Uncle Fred in the Springtime**" and "*The Cow-Creamer*"; and any other sums received by Mrs Wodehouse from the use as aforesaid of any other literary works of her husband.

b)   [*re Rose Elizabeth Rohmer*]

c)   Whether said sums were received by you from the user of such works to the direct credit of the wives, or received for the credit of the authors and then allocated by you on your books. If so, furnish the dates of allocations and the amounts thereof, and the payor of such amounts.

d)   The dates and amounts when the collections were remitted to the respective wives, the form of such remittance, and, if by check of your company, copies of the check, including the reverse side thereof.

e)   Whether your company received periodic instructions from the respective wives or husbands as to the dispositions of the collections, and, if so, furnish copies of such instructions.

It was evidently from the answers to these questions that the Judge in the Tax Court was able to decide to ignore the assignments to Ethel because although, as indicated above, there was meticulous attention to form, "No notices were given to the publishing company which bought the stories. This fact showed there was no real donative intent, the gift was ineffective ... " This did, at least mean there was no liability to gift tax! Not even the IRS would claim on the one hand that there was no gift, and on the other hand, there was a gift tax liability. Or would they?

As a result of their review, the IRS decided to argue first, that no tax returns had been filed for 1923 and 1924, and secondly that there were substantial understatements of taxable income from

1937 to 1941 (1939 excepted). The approximate amount of the resulting claims were $ 10,000 for 1923 and 1924, including penalties, and some $ 45,000 for 1937 to 1941.

The reader will not be surprised to learn that Wodehouse made some trenchant comments to his friend Bill Townend (30 May, 1945) on learning about this development:

> Another difficulty is that I am once more having trouble with the American income tax people. They have now dug back to 1923 — 22 years! — and claimed that I made no return that year. My argument is that I must have done, as I was in New York that year and left on a liner, and you can't leave on a liner unless you've paid your tax. I suppose the thing will drag on and on and eventually we shall reach some compromise.

At this time, Wodehouse had naturally become somewhat out of touch with the day-to-day life of his readers, whether in the US or the UK, and the conditions in which they may be living. He was thus not in a position to fully reflect these conditions in the detail of his writing, as Reynolds jnr. indicated in a letter of 14 June, 1945:

> ... I think it should be perfectly clear that the stories are of England today, or rather what we assume to be changed England. Of course, I'm not trying to suggest that you write realism — the genius of your novels is not because of their realism — but we Americans broadly assume the rich in England have almost no money, due to the income tax, that the kinds of food are very limited, an enormous number of buildings in London are destroyed etc ... etc ..., a story that assumes the case but is a humorous story around people, would have a lot of appeal.

This period of his life was confusing, as he was not sure of the market for which he should try to write. On 30 June, 1945, he wrote to Townend:

At present, however, I take but a faint interest in the American market, as the US Government is claiming this large sum of money from me for income tax and would infallibly pouch anything I made over there. My case comes up in September, and I suppose will end, as before, in my paying about a tenth of what they claim. As the year now in dispute is 1921 and all my records have been lost and also, one imagines, all those of the Government, I don't see how any conclusion can be arrived at except a compromise.

Wodehouse seems to have decided that if possible he would prefer to live in the US when the war was over, particularly as no confirmation was given that there would be no prosecution if he returned to the UK. But he did remain concerned about his tax position, and wrote to Guy Bolton on 17 July, 1945:

I wonder if the American Authorities would facilitate my coming over if I put it up to them that I wanted to be on the spot to clean up our income tax dispute.

Soon afterwards, on 13 August, 1945, Reynolds Jnr wrote to Wodehouse:

... I am of the firm opinion that I can sell your material although I am afraid not at the prices that you used to get ... it might be wiser to wait until the tax matter has come to a head which will be within the next few months.

This was a prediction showing a considerable lack of experience in matters of tax administration.

Just a month later, on 13 September, 1945, Wodehouse wrote to Townend:

I don't know why, but I am enjoying life amazingly these days.   Thunderclouds fill the sky in every direction, including a demand for $ 120,000 from the US income tax people (case starts on Monday unless they settle it in advance) but I continue to be happy. After all, there has been a distinct improvement since a year ago.

As mentioned in Chapter 6, another British author, Sax Rohmer, had also decided to take on the might of the IRS. He had sought to argue that, where a lump sum was received for the sale of first and second American and Canadian serial rights in a book written by a nonresident alien, who retained the other rights, the lump sum was received from the sale of personal property and was not within the charge to tax provided for in the tax law. The IRS, and the Tax Court, believed that it should be subjected to tax.

The dispute arose from a change in the provisions of the law in the Revenue Act of 1936. Non-resident aliens were made subject to 15% tax on a range of sources of income including dividends, rents, salaries, ... or other ... determinable annual or periodical gains, profits or income. Note that the term "royalties" was not specifically included on the list. But the Courts were able to point to precedent and the IRS successfully argued that the definition of taxable income must include royalties.

This did not by itself allow the IRS to walk away with the decision, however, for Rohmer was arguing, through Watson Washburn, that the receipt of a lump-sum for the sale *in toto* of a specific part of an author's bundle of rights under his copyright was not a receipt of royalties but of proceeds from the sale of personal property. The Court looked at the Sabatini case but noted that there were some differences not only in the facts, but also in the wording of the applicable law.

In coming to their conclusion, the Court considered the history of the specific piece of law they were interpreting (a normal and valid procedure in the US). In the UK (ie, Rohmer's country), this would not have been permitted at the time under any circumstances. Even today, it would take some exceptional confusion in the wording of the law for the Courts to take into account any part of the Parliamentary debate concerning the purpose of the legislation. And should a taxpayer be treated in any event as if such a complex matter were bed-time reading when he would not realistically have had a practical means of accessing the background notes?

In any event, the Court concluded that amendments to the law made in 1936 were designed to eliminate US tax on capital gains realised by non-resident aliens. (This was a pragmatic change in the law, because it had been found impractical to collect tax assessed in these circumstances.) It then used this conclusion to bolster its decision that a payment for a licence should be taxed as income, as otherwise it would escape taxation, and confirmed the tax assessments on Rohmer.

They then took a very impractical approach with respect to a minor part of the case, again on a point which was relevant to Wodehouse's. Rohmer's income had been received in part from magazines with Canadian sales, and US tax was not payable on the proportion of income attributable to Canadian rights. It was thus necessary to make an allocation of the receipts between those attributable to the US rights and those attributable to the Canadian.

The Court said that as there was no direct evidence of how much had been paid for the Canadian rights, they could not permit any of the receipts to be attributed to Canada. Such a lily-livered judgment does not meet with this writer's approval, any more than it would have met with Rohmer's. Evidence as to the relative circulations of the magazines in the US and Canada was offered, as was testimony about the level of fees paid by some magazines for Canadian serial rights of lesser authors. The courts do not earn a single point out of ten for effort in relation to this aspect of the case. They did not seem to appreciate that justice can require the application of pragmatism and common-sense in some circumstances.

The Rohmer decision was a blow to Wodehouse, but not a surprise. As he wrote to Guy Bolton on 9 January, 1946, (just six days after the decision was given):

> Talking of the Treasury and my tax trouble, Washburn has just written that the court has just decided unfavourably what is known as the Sax Rohmer appeal — that is to say, alien authors do have to pay tax on the sale in America of serial rights and cannot laugh things off by claiming that they are lump sales. I must say I'm not surprised. I am pretty optimistic by nature, but I never expected that my entire income for the last 20 years would turn out not to have been subject to tax after all! All I hope is that what seems to be the quite illegal claims the Government are making on me will be decided in my favour. I wish they would hurry up and come to a decision.

The earlier part of this letter had revealed Wodehouse's continuing sensitivity to tax, and the need not to be found doing the wrong thing. He was trying to reach agreement with Guy Bolton on the split of the fee for the lyric *Bill*:

> ...According to Washburn my $ 2,000 will have to be paid into the US Treasury on account of my tax liabilities "subject to refund later if you win your case" (what a hope!). So I am wondering if it is too late for you to take the whole lot and with my share include me in on the purchase of the **Oh Boy** picture rights, a sporting venture which I am all for. Probably this would turn out to be a conspiracy against the Treasury, so perhaps we had better let the thing ride. Let the blighters collar the $ 2,000 and I will get Washburn to pay my share of the **Oh Boy** picture rights when the time comes.

He had evidently found a sympathetic ear and wrote again to Bolton on 6 April, 1946:

> It really is awful the way one's money goes these days. Last week I got a dividend warrant on some English stock, and the amount was £ 43 15s. Against these figures was the statement that £ 43 15s had been deducted at source for income tax. One knew in a vague sort of way that income tax was at ten bob in the pound, but somehow it was a shock to see it in black and white. As I am a non-resident, I believe this dough will eventually be refunded, but only after I've spent a fortune on an accountant who will have to keep after them for months.

And again to Bolton on 19 May, 1946:

> When I went to the US Embassy to get my visa, I was told that owing to what has happened it would be necessary in my case to make investigations and refer the matter to Washington....I am hoping the visa will go through all right. If it doesn't I'm afraid I shall be stymied. But it seems to me that as I shall shortly hear from the US Government that I owe them a good bit of money on that Income Tax case and as their only hope of getting it is to let me come to America and make it, they will let me through.

In case you think Bill Townend was being ignored, you will be pleased to read that he also received a letter on the same topic, on 22 May, 1946:

> With any luck I could have four shows on Broadway next season. And now the US Embassy people are making difficulties about giving me a visa! They say they must first make enquiries in London to find out the facts in my case and will then consult Washington. Mind you, I think it will all end well and I shall get the visa, my ace of trumps being the fact that the US

Government is expecting to collect a wad of money from me for back income tax and their only hope is to let me come over and earn it. But the suspense is trying.

And it remained trying for a lot longer than Wodehouse would have liked. He finally got his visa and sailed for the US on 18 April, 1947. Remarkably, this was just three weeks after the first Tax Court hearing that took place, the Court noting with sympathy the reasons for his absence. After such a long delay, one would have thought the hearing could have been further postponed to await the arrival of the only witness who was in a position to give evidence on a number of relevant and crucial factual matters!

But one must guard against the temptation of jumping ahead of oneself. There were several further complaining, or resigned, letters to be written by Wodehouse to his friends before he was in a position to leave France.

First, to Guy Bolton, on 28 July, 1946:

I am hoping that by the time I am ready to come over my income tax case will have been settled. At present I am in the unpleasant position of having everything I make in America impounded and held in escrow or whatever it is and I would very much like to get this straightened out before I arrive. Washburn was expecting the Tax Court's decision in June, but nothing has broken yet. I am hoping that at the worst I shall get off with the payment of the $ 30,000 which the Government trousered at the outset.

His continued concern with tax, and in particular the rates of tax, was next in evidence in a letter to Bill Townend on 27 August, 1946:

157

I don't understand servant conditions in England. Lady Deterding, who owns this flat, at **36** Boulevard Souchet, Paris, has just let her house near Ascot out at £ 4,000 a year with an option to buy at £ 150,000. In other words, it must be a place which needs a staff of about **20**. And where does anyone get the money nowadays for that? I wouldn't have thought that with the present taxation it would be possible to make much more that £ 4,000 a year. But I suppose all these rich people are living on their capital.

He continued in this vein, with a different example, in a letter of 24 January, 1947, to Guy Bolton:

How do you feel about making money these days? It seems to me that one ought to strive to keep one's income down to a figure which will allow one to live comfortably and resist any invitations to increase it. The *Daily Mail* here has just published a table showing how much you actually get to keep of your money in England these days. The fellow who earns £ 5,000 gets £ 2,413. The £ 10,000 bloke gets £ 3,488. But the poor sap who has been chump enough to work really hard and make £ 50,000 a year finds himself with £ 4,963. So after killing himself trying to strip the rival who makes £ 10,000 per annum he only scoops in about £ 1,500 more than him. I'm damned if I see how England can ever expect to recover as long as this goes on. What on earth is the sense of pleading with people to work harder if by making £ 50,000 a year you're only a trifle better off than if you satisfied yourself with £ 10,000 and took it easy.

This sums up, very concisely, the thoughts of many in the UK throughout the first thirty-five or forty years after the second world war, until top tax rates were reduced to more acceptable rates during the 1980s.

During the 1970s, while those top tax rates in the UK were at 98%, the **Financial Times** published a reader's letter complaining about an increase in the cost of the newspaper. It pointed out that, now the price per daily edition had risen to 10p, the weekly cost was 60p [no issue on Sundays] and the annual cost £ 31.20. As this was paid out of taxed income, the true cost in pre-tax income was £ 1,560 per annum.

The writer went on to say that he was a substantial shareholder in the company for which he worked and of which he was the chief executive, and the yield of the annual dividend compared to the stock market price was 5%. He was therefore holding shares with a market value of £ 31,200 merely to obtain sufficient income to enable him to buy his daily paper!

He also offered a solution to his problem. He arranged for the company to buy the paper.

As a result, the company would obtain a tax deduction for the annual cost of £ 31.20, and he would be able to free up shares to the value of £ 31,200!

(It would be interesting to know whether Messrs Nicolson and Duff Cooper would have taken exception to this action. Probably, but not if they had thought of it themselves.)

The Tax Court eventually gave its decision on the various aspects of the Wodehouse tax position on 28 March, 1947. It was a highly complex affair, but the next few pages seek to provide a flavour of what the dispute was about. To bring to the fore some part of the anger and indignation that the litigants must have been feeling, readers may like to imagine that they have themselves been in the position of the Wodehouses, and may care to contemplate the extensive travel and varied and trying circumstances of the previous twenty years. The subject matter for 1923 and 1924, and their attempt to assert fraud in relation to 1937, really do suggest that some in the IRS lived in the fantasy world of Cloud-cuckoo-land.

To recapitulate, the IRS had chosen first to claim that no tax returns had been filed for 1923 and 1924. In fact, the cases for 1923 and 1924 were swiftly and finally dealt with. The only point really at issue was — did he file tax returns for those years?

While putting yourself in the Wodehouse position, do bear in mind the lack of technological assistance for making and keeping copies of documents some 70 years ago.

How would you react today to a suggestion that you had not filed some official forms in 1970?

How would you start to prove that you did file them?

Even if there were publicly available photocopying facilities in 1970, how many people would have used them?

And of course there were no such things in 1924.

Even if you had been in a position to make copies at the time, for how long would you have kept them?

Especially if you had moved house several times, had lived for a fair period in each of the US, the UK and France, had been interned in Germany during a world war, and had had your house occupied by soldiers and your belongings ransacked?

One might reasonably assume that Wodehouse, or anyone else, could be exonerated from culpability for not having readily available copies of twenty-year old tax returns. But the problem was, that, *incredibly, under the US litigation system, which would apply equally today, **he would have to bear the principal burden of proof that he had indeed filed those returns!***

Rumsey, Wodehouse's agent at the time, might have been the first hope. But he had ceased to act in 1926, and when, more than a decade later his business declined and he moved to smaller premises (in 1938), he threw away virtually all his pre-1931 papers. Not an outrageous or unreasonable action of an irresponsible man.

His counsel, Watson Washburn, decided that the obvious course — and perhaps the only one offering any chance of success — was to explore what records were available to the Internal Revenue themselves, and he applied for subpoenas directed to the collectors of Internal Revenue for the relevant districts of New York, requiring them to produce the tax returns for Wodehouse, Rumsey (who had filed withholding tax returns for Wodehouse) and the American Play Co for 1918 to 1924, together with accompanying papers.

So what was the outcome? Was there, as in most of his novels, to be a happy ending, with the IRS admitting to having made a mistake and withdrawing the tax assessments? Well, yes and no. Or to be precise, yes, no and yes. There was a happy ending, and the tax assessments were withdrawn. But no mistake was admitted.

IRS deputy collectors, who had made the decision to litigate and make the claim that no returns had been filed, were present to give evidence at the trial, but refused to testify "without the express permission of the Commissioner of Internal Revenue on penalty of dismissal". One of the deputy collectors had made no attempt to obtain the necessary permission and the other claimed to have had no opportunity to do so. When the Court directed each of the deputy collectors to answer a question, each declined to do so "in view of his instructions". Whereas it was easy to conclude that Wodehouse could be exonerated from culpability for not producing the required evidence, the same could not be said for the tax collectors, who seem to have made no attempt whatsoever to support their claims.

All the IRS would offer in evidence were "certificates", not under seal, purporting to show that various revenue offices which had been contacted had no record of any filing of the returns for those years. These "certificates" were not admitted in evidence.

Fortunately for Wodehouse, there had been developed in the *Capento Securities Corporation* case[1] a general doctrine of US law, which still applies, that:

When a party fails to produce documentary evidence pursuant to a notice to produce and no satisfactory explanation for such failure is given, an inference may properly be recognised that the evidence would be unfavorable to the party failing to produce it.

The Judge concluded:

[The IRS] ... may have in [its] possession the documentary evidence which might have proved conclusively — and without the aid of the additional evidence of record — that the petitioner, or someone acting for him, did file the returns in question. Therefore, the only conclusion justified by this state of facts is that the respondent's files and records would have proved [Wodehouse's] contention.

He also pointed out the irony — which would surely not have been lost on Wodehouse — that the 1933 settlement had followed a thorough review of the files, had covered a period starting in 1925, and yet had made no mention of 1923 or 1924. Readers will recall Wodehouse's own comment, that he left New York on a liner during that period (indeed he left the US in each of 1923, 1924 and 1925), and he couldn't have done that unless he was up to date with his tax returns.

So, a happy ending in respect of 1923 and 1924.

Digressing for a moment, Paul Revere Reynolds was subpoenaed to appear before the Tax Court in New York on 6 October, 1947, (six months after the main Tax Court hearing) and was required to take with him:

> All books, records and contracts of any kind of the firm of Paul R Reynolds or of Paul R Reynolds and Son, 599 Fifth Ave., New York City, relating to the disposition of literary properties or rights therein on behalf of the author Pelham G Wodehouse, for which payments were received during the calendar years 1921 and 1922, and showing the names of the purchasers and the amounts paid in 1921 and 1922 by the purchasers of such literary properties or rights therein in acquiring the same.

Whether there was a hearing on that date is unclear. Certainly Wodehouse in his letters referred to these years as well as 1923 and 1924, so it was more than a passing problem. The upshot seems to have been that either no assessments were actually raised, or if they were they were dismissed.

But now what about the later years?

The disputes for 1938 to 1941 all concentrated on a number of technical issues but the matter of greatest concern was the claim that there was "fraud" in 1937. No matter the angle from which one looks at it, an accusation of "fraud" is unpleasant. The burden of proving fraud was on the IRS, and if they failed to do so any technical issues for that year became irrelevant, because the statute of limitations would have prevented the IRS from assessing to tax income from a year so long past.

The transaction which had caught the eye of the IRS has already been touched on — it was the formation of SwissCo, which on April 26, 1934 bought from Wodehouse for $ 400,000, all his earnings, copyrights, royalties, commissions and other revenue from the sale of his literary, theatrical or cinematographic productions in North America, South America and Canada for a term of 4 years. The agreement incorporated a list of 28 relevant productions already in existence but was also to encompass rights during the four year period for works yet to be produced.

Despite his earlier administrative lapses, Wodehouse's former agent, Rumsey, had been recommended in May 1934 to SwissCo as a prospective agent to handle past and future productions, and this appointment was duly made. Rumsey dealt with either SwissCo or Mr Weinbren, the accountant acting for SwissCo, in relation to Wodehouse's literary activities.

Evidence was accepted that a number of publishers, and the Reynolds Agency, were told of the agreement and that proceeds should in future be paid to SwissCo. Furthermore, it should be noted that the IRS was aware of, and already investigating, the SwissCo transaction as early as June 9, 1935. It apparently became a factor in the compromise negotiated in 1936 although it is difficult to see how, since this settlement covered the years 1925 to 1933, and SwissCo was not formed until 1934.

SwissCo filed US tax returns for 1934 to 1937, claiming refunds of tax withheld at source from payments made to it, and although not all the claims were accepted, by December 6, 1940 (in respect of 1934 and 1935) and March 18, 1941 (in respect of 1936 and 1937) its tax position for those years had been agreed, and as indicated in the previous chapter, a refund had been received following the audit for 1937.

Despite their evident awareness, at least from 1935, about the existence and activities of SwissCo, during which period they apparently accepted its tax returns for each of the four years of its active life, it was not until 18 June, 1943, that the IRS considered making Wodehouse's representatives aware that in their view the transactions involving SwissCo were all parts of a fraudulent scheme devised to evade the payment of his "just income taxes then due (or to become due on his subsequent earnings)".

Whatever the merits of the IRS technical arguments, to this author, writing as a person whose entire professional career has been spent considering business tax issues in the UK and internationally, the fraud claim represents an unacceptable abuse of language. It is unacceptable today, and it would have been every bit as unacceptable in the 1940s.

It seems that the IRS were given substantial information about SwissCo at an early date. They had withholding tax returns in relation to payments to SwissCo in respect of 1934 and later years. As discussed in chapter 2, tax evasion through "fraud" in generally accepted tax parlance implies hiding either relevant facts, the existence of companies, the existence of sources of income or the existence of transactions from the Revenue authorities. The amount of information available to the IRS, and the fact that tax returns had been filed by SwissCo and fully and finally audited by the IRS themselves, makes it very difficult to see how this charge could have been justified.

It is not, and no-one should ever consider it to be, fraudulent to say to Revenue authorities anywhere:

> *Look, I've arranged these transactions and I think the effect is to make me exempt from tax, because ..., but if you prove to my satisfaction, or the Courts decide, that I am wrong, I will pay the amount due with interest.*

The authorities may not like it.

They are entitled to challenge you.

They may even change the law prospectively or retrospectively.

But what they cannot do is successfully allege fraud when nothing has been hidden from the Revenue and nothing has been done intentionally to mislead the Revenue.

165

So it is a very great pleasure to report that the Judge agreed with this sentiment with these simple but forthright words:

The respondent [IRS] has not proved his charge of fraud.

It is an unfortunate fact that an accusation of tax fraud, like mud, sticks in the minds of those who care little for facts, or had made up their minds — and commented — before the case was settled. The modern American philosophy ("If it moves, sue it") had evidently not taken hold in 1947, or at least not in the mind of a British citizen still living in France. A pity in some ways, as the injudicious language which had been used about him might have provided Wodehouse with a plentiful and continuing source of tax-free receipts!

With the problems of 1937 summarily dealt with, it is time to move on to the technically more meaty but overall less damning issues of 1938, 1940 and 1941. There was no suggestion of culpable wrongdoing in respect of the disputes for these years — only questions as to whose interpretation of the law relating to those issues were correct.

There were four such issues, of which the first three were interrelated:

a whether the receipt of lump-sums for serials which were sold to **Saturday Evening Post** and **Cosmopolitan** was taxable as income, or exempt from tax as capital. [It was over this question that Wodehouse expressed himself so forcibly to Bill Townend in his letters (see eg, pages 176 and 178), querying how any government could be so loony as to think that these receipts might be anything but income.]

Readers will be able to recognise the questions asked and answered in the Sabatini and Rohmer cases, and may think that Wodehouse had little chance of success where they had failed.

b   whether, if the IRS won the argument in (a), some of the income could be regarded as foreign source income and exempt, since the sale transferred rights to the Canadian and South American markets as well as the US market. Again, the decision in the Rohmer case could not have filled Wodehouse with confidence about the outcome.

c   if amounts in (a) proved to be taxable, which of PG and Ethel Wodehouse was to be taxed in relation to payments received for serial rights to novels and other works of which he was the author in circumstances in which he had gifted her certain rights to a half-share in the work.

d   whether he could validly claim a deduction for attorney's fees.

One cannot be sure that all the public records relating to these cases have been traced. However, the author is aware that these four points were the subject of a total of at least six hearings before various Courts, and the development of the legal argument depended on some occasions on the prior outcomes. Perhaps the most constructive approach is to set out a timetable of the various Court Hearings, and the points which they covered, before guiding the reader along the various tracks to home:

1947

March 28   Tax Court heard points -

              (a) for 1938, 1940 and 1941
              (b) for 1938, 1940 and 1941
              (c) for 1938 and 1940
              (d) for 1938, 1940 and 1941.

1948

March 16   Appeals Court, Fourth Circuit, heard point (a) for 1938 and 1941 only. As it found in favour of PGW it did not need to consider points (b) and (c) at this time.

December 10   Supreme Court heard point (a) for 1938 and 1941, reversing the Fourth Circuit and finding for the IRS. Accordingly, they sent the case back to the Fourth Circuit Appeals Court to hear points (b) and (c).

(The result of this hearing was not given until June 13, 1949, adding to the Wodehouses' irritation.)

1949

November 21   Appeals Court, Second Circuit, heard points (a), (b) and (c) for 1940.

December 21   The Fourth Circuit heard points (b) and (c) for 1938, and (b) for 1941. Since the Court found in favour of Wodehouse, in principle, on matter (b), the case had to be sent back to the Tax Court for the impact of their decision to be evaluated.

1950

December 6   The Tax Court determined the factual allocation required in respect of point (b) for 1938 and 1941, but did not need to do so for 1940.

It would not be meaningful to spend any time on point (d) which was found in Wodehouse's favour by the Tax Court and not appealed by the IRS. But the other matters have points of interest, and certainly justify the frustration which Wodehouse showed with the US tax system. The eventual outcome certainly warrants the tag of loony, and it is no wonder that he gently satirised the tax authorities at every opportunity thereafter.

A little background to the relevant US law needs to be provided for the benefit of those who have not yet tackled the Appendix.

In common with tax authorities the world over, the IRS delight in providing complexity, choice and temptation to their unwilling customers. For US citizens, the options include the right to file tax returns as married couples, which in turn carries the right to claim two personal exemptions and charge a greater amount of income to tax at the lower tax rates. The effect of this is to calculate the family tax bill as though both members had equal amounts of income, and is similar, though still superior, to the system which since 1990 has applied in the UK.

But this option was not and is still not available for aliens, resident or non-resident, which was the status which P G Wodehouse retained in the US until 1955, when he took out US citizenship. Even this simple statement is complicated by the fact that in some states in the US there is (and was) the concept of Community Property status. This says that in any family, between the husband and wife, half of what's yours is mine, and half of what's mine is yours. [It is understood that this has been effectively extended beyond formal family relationships in recent years, but any writer who has not studied this in detail will get into hot water by trying to be more specific].

From a tax point of view, the big benefit for those in Community Property states who were not able to file as a couple of married US citizens, was that each partner was able to claim half the income received in the year, and thus be in a similar position to

169

two US citizens when it came to shelling out the tax payments to the IRS. (The law has since been amended to change this analysis in relation to earnings.)

And so it was that PGW, as red-blooded an Englishman who ever believed that the American government would waste any contributions he might make to their coffers, had gone to Hollywood for a year in Autumn 1936, determined to hold on to as much as possible of what was his. Initially, he filed his tax return as a resident alien on a Community Property basis, as he had spotted or been advised that California was a Community Property status State.

Washburn, his attorney, had queried at the time whether it was appropriate to regard himself as resident for that year merely on the basis that his "Quota" visa entitled him to that status, but offered an alternative justification for the basis of filing. Washburn suggested that as France also recognised the concept of Community Property, if he was a French resident for tax purposes, this would validate the tax return beyond doubt.

Clearly, the idea that he should in some way be treated on a similar basis to US citizens for the period of his residence in the US had been well ingrained in Wodehouse's thinking when he had consulted Washburn next, in Autumn 1937. This time, the advice received was more complicated, but included the suggestion that the right to file tax returns on a Community Property basis would be influenced by his tax status in England, where there is no concept of Community Property, and he should check this forthwith. This was accompanied by a suggestion that the same result could be achieved if he made an outright gift to Ethel of a half-interest in various works **before** any income was derived from them.

On his return to England he was advised that he remained tax domiciled in England, an unhelpful outcome from a US tax point of view, with the implication that community property returns might not be valid. This led to two further steps — first, amended tax returns were filed, for each of PG and Ethel, he having substantial extra tax to pay, and she obtaining a refund. Secondly, the alternative plan — no doubt plan B — was activated.

Accordingly, on January 3, 1938, Ethel had received an assignment of an undivided one-half interest in various rights to **The CowCreamer**[2], and on September 1, 1938, received a similar assignment of rights to **Uncle Fred in the Springtime**[3]. Over a year later, on December 1, 1939, she received an assignment of rights to **Quick Service**[4].

The IRS chose to argue that these assignments, although perfectly proper in form, were designed solely to prevent the taxation of all PGW's income as his. As the Judge in the Tax Court said:

> *It is axiomatic that a taxpayer may take all proper measures to reduce his tax liability. The question is, "Were the measures proper?"*

While acknowledging the frankness with which the reasons underlying the assignments were explained to the Court, the Judge pointed out that in the absence of direct testimony from the Wodehouses (said to be a difficult thing to arrange as they were both still in France), the only motivating purpose brought to the attention of the Court was to divide the tax burden with his wife and so reduce the aggregate amount of taxes. There is a certain lack of credibility in the comments concerning the Wodehouses' absence, since they were sailing for America within a month! The Judge added a few more comments before deciding that the assignments "lacked the merit of reality" and found in favour of the IRS. He also followed the Sax Rohmer decision in holding that lump-sums received for serial rights were to be included in taxable income.

A straw poll taken of the population at large (in England, this is referred to as "the view of the man on the Clapham omnibus" or "the opinion of the shopkeeper in Cleckheaton") would surely have felt that this was a fair outcome, and that should be the end of the matter.

But no. Wodehouse was advised to appeal, on this and other issues, and so was immersed in an anachronistic quirk of US jurisdiction.

The 1938 and 1941 appeals were set to be heard by the Court of Appeals for the Fourth Circuit in March 1948, while the 1940 appeal was to be heard by the Court of Appeals of the Second Circuit at a later date.

But this is where the reader is left in suspense, waiting impatiently to find out how many more corpses will appear and wondering whether he can find out whodunnit if he turns to page 236, while the other matters on which the Tax Court gave their opinion are reviewed. The Tax Court found for the IRS on both points (a) and (b), following the *Sax Rohmer* case, as well as on point (c), relating to the gift to Ethel.

When discussing the Sax Rohmer case, it was suggested that the Court's finding on point (b) was unimaginative in view of the evidence concerning the circulation of the various journals which was available to the Court. It would not have been a huge step to take to assume that a *pro rata* portion of the fee received by Wodehouse could be allocated to Canada, and thus be exempt from US taxes. The information before the Tax Court in the Wodehouse case, concerning the net average paid circulation for the relevant magazines, is shown on page 170, and the point seems self-evident.

From subsequent correspondence it is difficult to believe that Wodehouse had a full understanding of the decisions. First, on 12 April, 1947, he wrote to Townend:

> Thank goodness my American income tax trouble has been settled after dead silence on the part of the Tax Courts since October 1945. What happened was that the tax people suddenly got the idea that I had not paid taxes for 1921 to 1925, if you can imagine it, and also

172

COMPARATIVE CIRCULATIONS WITHIN CANADA AND USA

		CIRCULATION		
Wodehouse contribution	6 months ending	United States	Canada	Other Foreign
SATURDAY EVENING POST				
None	31.12.37	3,037,562	*	189,867
The CowCreamer	30. 6.38	3,095,355	*	191,228
Uncle Fred in the Springtime	31.12.38	3,061,009	139,739	54,985
None	30. 6.39	3,104,208	146,002	52,648
None	31.12.39	3,130,396	148,163	52,230
Quick Service	30. 6 40	3,231,496	153,291	52,196
None	30. 6.41	3,328,875	121,307	43,019
Money in the Bank	30.12.41	3,425,025	122,049	57,546
COSMOPOLITAN				
None	30. 6.41	1,850,014	41,705	21,618
My Years Behind Barbed Wire	31.12.41	1,961,600	49,436	24,164
* Included in Other Foreign				

kicked about my splitting my income with Ethel. They impounded about $ 39,000 of mine. The Court now decided that I did pay tax in the years mentioned (as of course I did, only naturally all records have been destroyed years ago), but upheld the tax people as regards splitting with Ethel. The net result is that I have to pay about $ 20,000 which means a refund of about $ 19,000, and the extraordinary thing is that instead of mourning over the lost $ 20,000 I am feeling frightfully rich as if I had just been left $ 19,000 by an uncle in Australia. I find nowadays that any money these Governments allow one to keep seems like money earned. Anyway my whole financial position in America has changed overnight, and instead of landing without a penny and having to make a quick touch from Doubleday or someone I have become self-supporting. It is a tremendous relief.

He followed this up with another letter, dated 11 May, when he was still full of his victory:

Owing to the US Government refunding most of the money they pinched from me in 1943, I am in funds and don't really need the magazines. (Ye Gov't are slipping me about $ 20,000 and, what is more, paying interest on it for four years at 6%, which will be a nice bit of extra stuff.) Washburn thinks, too, that when we appeal we may get all the money they impounded. I won my case on all counts except one, viz they ruled that when I split my income with Ethel I couldn't do that here and said the total tax was due to me, which put me in a high bracket as the period covered included the opulent year in Hollywood.

On 25 May, 1947, he wrote to Guy Bolton:

I forgot to to tell you. My tiff with Mr Whiskers is ended and he is refunding me about $ 20,000 plus interest at 6% since 1943. It is just like finding money. I had kissed that $ 40,000 good-bye. I won on every count except that in 1937 they decided that I was not entitled to split my income with Ethel, so they're sticking to half the $ 40,000 because of that, though my lawyer seems to think I might win on appeal.

The last sentence — like some of the comments in the letters to Townend — is blatantly wrong, and suggests either a sense of bravado, a genuine misunderstanding, or the mere use of a faulty memory in writing a letter to a friend and not bothering to check the facts. He did **NOT** win on any significant count, **except** the critical one in relation to accusations of fraud so the 1937 assessments failed. Apart from that — the most significant point necessary to establish his honesty — he only won the consolation prize of a deduction for attorneys' fees.

His comment that he was not entitled to split income with Ethel in 1937 was particularly inept — as he did not assign any literary properties over to her until 1938! And he won the 1937 case in full, without detailed consideration of any of the technical issues.

It must have been a little boring for Townend to be told about the progress, or lack of progress, of the tax case, time and time again, with recapitulations being offered in each letter. In December 1947, before any of the appeals had come to be heard, there is another letter to Townend. It starts by referring to a new project he planned to get into with Scott Meredith, for flooding the market with cheap editions:

> This has been postponed. In other words our capital was not enough, and rather than put up more — which we couldn't have done at the moment — we thought it best to wait a year, by which time, Scott thinks, printing costs will have gone down, income tax will have been reduced, etc.

But he can't resist adding comments about his ongoing tax problem, of which only the first sentence or two was in any way interesting:

> My financial position now is maddening and tantalising. In England I have all the money there is except for a few quid which Anthony Mildmay and the Rothschilds have, but I can't touch it. Over here I am all right, but I have to watch expenses a bit for the moment. It is all tied up with this income tax trouble. In 1943 ye government pinched $ 40,000 of my money and put a lien on my funds, which means that nobody who owes me money can pay it. The case has come on and verdict so far is that I owe the government $ 20,000 on one count (we are appealing). The rest of the case has to do with my 1921 tax, which they say I didn't pay and plus interest and fines amounts to $ 28,000. So at

175

the worst they would stick to my remaining $ 20,000 and I should have to pay another $ 8,000. (I am sorry to have started all this dull stuff, but I got carried away. Be patient.)

BUT my lawyer thinks I am certain to win the second case, in which event I should be repaid my $ 20,000, Doubleday would then have to pay me the $ 15,000 which they owe me and Harms two or three thousand for music publishing. So at any moment I might be in the chips, with about $ 40,000 in my kick. But meanwhile there's the weary waiting, and I can't seem to click with magazines.

And so the scene moved to the Appeal Court of the Fourth Circuit to continue the saga by hearing the cases for 1938 and 1941 (but not for 1940), and this had the making of one of the television soaps of which Wodehouse later became so fond. The Fourth Circuit of the Appeal Court found in favour of Wodehouse on point (a). Unfortunately, since this decision was reversed in the Supreme Court, it is no longer included in the case record prints, and the writer has not been able to trace the rationale for that decision. But, as a result, the Court did not need to pronounce on points (b) and (c).

At this time, the IRS were by no means only after Wodehouse. He spotted an item in *Theatrical News* for 10 June, 1948, that the IRS were re-examining the tax returns in relation to a show that had been put on, claiming that the show's backers were a corporation, liable to corporate income tax, excess profits tax and the rest, and commented to Guy Bolton:

In a nutshell what it boils down to is this, if the Internal Revenue's case is upheld, bang it seems to me goes show business. No backer of a play would be able to deduct more than $ 1,000 from his income tax in the event of a flop, and, as the *Herald Tribune* says "In an industry in which the odds against the investor are so great, this could mean that no individual in his right mind would risk any more than the deductible $ 1,000 which in turn would mean that a producer would have to corral 200 different investors to put on a $ 200,000 show. Such financial acrobatting would be virtually impossible." Of course, these things always look at first worse than they really are and I don't think any Administration would dare to take a step which would bring show business to a standstill, but it's very disquieting.

His reducing pessimism was, however, evidenced by a letter on 7 September to Bill Townend:

Montgomery Ford, who was a manager before the war, has made an adaptation of my **Quick Service** and wants to put it on. But can he get the money? He thinks that once we have signed up a good director, it will be easy enough. I am hoping for the best. To me, the thought of raising $ 60,000 is an appalling one, but apparently New York is full of people who will risk two or three thousand dollars on a show, the attraction being that if the show flops they can deduct it from their income tax.

There is a certain naivety in this comment, apart from the fact that it is not wholly consistent with his letter to Guy Bolton only three months before. Many people, including the Revenue authorities, talk glibly about

writing it off against tax or

deduct it from their income tax

even today.

But that suggests a pound for pound, or dollar for dollar, reduction in a tax bill for the amount of money spent or lost. And that is wrong. Where a deduction for an expense or loss is allowed, it is offset not against the tax, but against the person's income. So when the tax is calculated, the person claiming the deduction only gets a tax saving equal to the rate of tax on that income. Ironically, the higher the top tax rate payable, the greater the value of relief for a tax deduction.

Some people know what they mean, and talk about writing something off against tax as a form of shorthand. Others seem to think that being able to write something off against tax is a panacea which cures all ills. To put Wodehouse's comments in perspective, one merely needs to bear in mind that if you invest in a show and lose money, you will still lose money after tax relief. Not as much, maybe, but a loss is still a loss.

Before looking at the next stage of the proceedings, it is important to remember that by 1938 Wodehouse was no longer a US resident and had filed his tax return as a non-resident alien. This took on a significant importance in the Supreme Court, which in a 21 page judgment, identified the problem to be decided as turning on the meaning of the expression

gross income from sources within the United States

as it appears in various enactments which at the time formed part of the tax code, and whether various advances for serialised books he had received fell within the definition.

As Wodehouse himself commented, common sense would suggest that the answer was **"YES, of course"**, but as has been seen in connection with the Sax Rohmer case, there had been a number of changes in the relevant law imposing taxes on non-resident aliens from 1934 to 1938. The tax rate had risen from 4% to 10%, but the scope of the charge had been reduced to eliminate from charge anything which could not have tax easily deducted from the payment at source.

Wodehouse's attorney argued that the changes made had inadvertently had the effect of exempting lump-sum payments made for the sale of an interest in property before it had been copyrighted. This became an issue in 1938 because he had filed a tax return as a resident alien in 1937, and until 1936 receipts of this type were expressly subject to a withholding tax as part of the rules for taxing non-resident alien individuals.

Becoming more technical, counsel for Wodehouse argued that the sum he received was in return for the sale of a property interest in a copyright, and not a payment of royalty for rights granted under protection of a copyright. The IRS countered by saying that PGW could not escape taxation of such receipts merely by showing that each payment was received by him in a lump-sum in advance for certain uses of copyright, instead of in several payments to be made at intermediate dates during the life of the copyright.

Wodehouse claimed in a letter to Townend of 24 October, 1948, that the IRS decision to take an appeal to the Supreme Court did not surprise him, and in view of Sax Rohmer that was probably true. But it is quite obvious from the letter that he was becoming steadily more Emsworthian in his inability to remember accurately even broad factual details:

> My tax troubles fall into three separate channels. They claim that I didn't pay my 1923 tax and there's this thing they've just appealed about and I'm bound to say that my sympathies are rather with the Government as regards C. You will scarcely credit it, but my lawyer induced the Circuit Court of Appeals or whatever its called to rule that *Saturday Evening Post* serials don't count as income!!! And I am hoping the Supreme Court will uphold this. When you sell a story to the *Post* they buy all rights in it and then release all rights except first American serial, so that this seems to make it a capital sale and so not taxable. If one can get away with this, it seems to me that one can get away with anything, but they do have to go by the strict letter of the law and that appears to consider the thing a capital sale.

Incidentally, this is the last lap. They can't appeal again if the Supreme Court goes against them.

The beauty of the thing from my point of view (and what is causing the Government such mental agony) is that, if the verdict goes in my favour, I can instantly claim back all the tax I paid through the years on *Post* serials. So, of course, can every other foreign author. Naturally this is giving the Government prostration.

[Again, this is likely to be a partially erroneous understanding of the position. It would only have been possible for him to claim a refund in respect of years he was not resident in the US, which were not time-barred, and which were after the change in law which took effect in about 1936. His ability to reclaim tax, therefore, bearing in mind that 1938, 1940 and 1941 were under review, and any attempt to have reopened 1937 would have been dismissed as out of time, would have been very limited.]

My lawyer seems to think I shall win both the 1921 and 1923 (sic) cases. If I don't I think the worst that can happen is that the Government will stick to $ 40,000 which they pinched from me in 1943. I don't think there will be any more to pay. If I win, of course, I shall get back my $ 40,000 plus interest at 6% since 1943 which will mean another $ 13,400.

It would all be very exciting if it didn't take so long. It is about a year since the 1921 case was tried. I personally look on that $ 40,000 as gone with the wind and if I do get it back it will be like coming into a fat legacy. But can you imagine them starting in on me for my 1921 tax? I can't prove I paid it and they can't prove I didn't. The only thing is that you couldn't leave America without having paid your income tax and I certainly left it in 1921 and 1922. Oh well!

[Oh well! indeed. As mentioned above there does not seem to be a record of an actual hearing for 1921 and 1922. So the fact that Wodehouse may have left America in those years may have been relatively unimportant. What is much more relevant is that he definitely left America in each of 1923, 1924 and 1925, all relevant to the years under consideration!]

The mechanics of agreeing tax returns in the US were obviously a source of much frustration and concern to Wodehouse. But they did provide occasional moments of humour, as described in a letter to Bill Townend on 15 January, 1949:

> I have just received from the US Treasury a cheque for $ 4,500. What it is and why they sent it I simply can't imagine. My lawyer says its something to do with repaid interest on my 1941 tax. But the thing doesn't make sense. The Government put a lien on my money and won't let Doubleday pay me what they owe me, and at the same time they send me this cheque. You would have thought they would have held on to it until the tax cases were settled.
>
> The more I have to do with Governments the less I understand them. The result of my case before the Supreme Court isn't out yet, but I can't see why there should have been a case at all. The point at issue is does the money I got for **Saturday Evening Post** serials count as income? Any normal person would say yes of course it does, but the Government is solemnly deliberating the point and it's quite possible that they will refund me all the money I have paid in tax on those serials.

But that mood did not last for long, and by the time he wrote again to Townend in May, 1949, he was back to the philosophical approach:

Incidentally, owing to this lien which the income tax people put on my money in 1943, I haven't had a penny from Doubleday for years. They owe me about $ 16,000 exclusive of the Pocket Book sales, so if my case is ever settled I shall get a nice boost to my account.

The Supreme Court hearing, in December 1948 (although not reported until June 1949), was only concerned with the question of whether lump sum payments were taxable as income, in 1938 and 1941, and it seems to have leaned over backwards to find a way of confirming that the receipts should be taxed. This it achieved, by the slender majority of 5 to 3, so it remitted the case back to the Fourth Circuit Appeal Court for consideration of the subordinate issues (b) and (c).

This was undoubtedly another blow, as from time to time Wodehouse seems to have convinced himself that, despite the lack of logic a win would mean, he was actually going to get the tax back. He reported the decision to Townend and Bolton with varying degrees of resignation, in letters of 20 June, 1949, and 21 June, 1949, respectively. To Townend:

One consolation about being a back number, as I now feel I am in the USA, is the reflection that money nowadays has ceased to mean anything. For instance, a bird named Skouras, head of Fox Films, last year scooped in $ 810,000. After paying Federal and State taxes he nets $ 62,000. And Betty Grable who made $ 200,000 gets $ 31,000. I think these huge taxes are heading countries straight for the poor house, because eventually the people who make very large incomes as the result of terrific personal effort, are going to tell you what's the use and go fishing instead of working. I tell you what makes me absolutely sick, though, and that is the way the tax people come down on some poor bloke who after years of poverty suddenly clicks with one novel or play.

All this is not bitterness at the result of that Supreme Court decision of mine, as I had been warned by my lawyer that I had better be prepared for the worst and I had more or less discounted it. I couldn't believe in my most optimistic moments that any Government would let me get away with the argument that **Saturday Evening Post** serials weren't income but were outright sales. The silver lining in the cloud is that I shan't have to pay out any dough, as ye Government pinched enough in 1943 to cover it. If I win the case about my 1921 income tax (on which they have been now brooding for 18 months though any ordinary person like you or me could have settled it overnight) I should get back quite a bit. If I lose that I get nothing but also pay nothing. So the agony isn't as bad as it would be if I had been called on to cough up the lump sum now.

And to Guy Bolton:

The blasted Supreme Court ruled against me (5-3) in the appeal on my income tax case. I had a feeling they would. If I had won I should have been able to get back about $ 30,000 of the money they pinched from me in 1943. My only consolation is that I shan't have to cough up any actual money as the chunk they pinched from me covers everything. But it's maddening to think that if the set up had been 4-4 instead of 5-3 I should have won as the lower court had decided in my favour.

During the various hearings, Wodehouse and his advisers obviously kept a weather eye on the ongoing tax position. He was resident in France in 1947, and residents of France were exempt from US tax on literary royalties. So, in formal terms, Wodehouse provided the following certificate to Reynolds on 12 March, 1948:

I, P. G. Wodehouse, the undersigned, hereby certify as follows:

183

I reside at Pavillon Henri Quatre, St. Germain-En-Laye, Seine et Oise, France, and have had such residence during the calendar year 1947.

I had no permanent establishment in the United States at any time during the calendar year 1947.

The payment of royalties by you to me or the receipt by you for my account, of royalties on literary property of mine during 1947 is exempt from United States income tax under the provisions of Article VII of the Tax Convention between the United States and France.

Wodehouse continued to have a concern about the well-being of Bill Townend, and on 21 July, 1949, he wrote:

Have you finished the new book yet? I'm afraid it looks as though you and I would be pretty badly hit by all this trouble. I never can understand how, with income tax at nine bob [ie, nine shillings] in the pound, anyone has enough money to buy a book.

He returned to one of his pet themes of recent years in October, again in a letter to Townend:

What a hideous mess the Labour Government have got England into. And I suppose they will be re-elected next year. The thing I ask myself is this. If a man making £ 100,000 a year can only get as much for himself as a man who is making £ 10,000 a year, what inducement is there for him to sweat himself to the bone. And it is the £ 100,000 a year men who actually make a country's prosperity.

And then, a joyous letter to Townend, dated 5 November, 1949:

I have just had a very fat cheque from Doubledays for royalties on my last five books, held up because the income tax people had put a lien on my money.

Remarkable timing! Just three weeks before the next appeal was to be heard, and the lien is taken off! Are Governments loony after all?

During November and December, 1949, all the cases relating to 1940 were heard before the Second Circuit Appeal Court, and the Fourth Circuit Appeal Court heard the case resubmitted by the Supreme Court, on issues (b) and (c) for 1938 and 1941. The Second Circuit Judges made what is often referred to as a robust judgment, reversing the opinion of the Tax Court by a majority of two to one, and allowing the gift to Ethel (point (c)) to be treated as effective. The Judge giving the leading opinion considered that there was no understanding when the gift was made that despite the formal transfer the donor was to retain dominion over the property conveyed. He went on:

The only evidence in the record from which such an understanding might be inferred is the fact that Mr Wodehouse sent the manuscript to the literary agent who customarily acted for him in making contracts with publishers. That agent however was advised of the assignment and instructed to send Mrs Wodehouse her half of the proceeds of any contract he negotiated. Whether Mr Wodehouse consulted with his wife before transmitting the manuscript to the literary agent does not appear. If he did, her acquiescence in his proposal to have the literary agent dispose of their serial rights would not be sufficient to infer that they had previously agreed that he should retain control of the half interest purportedly conveyed to her. Nor do we think such an inference would be justified even if it be assumed that he did not consult her. A husband may be so certain that his wife will follow his advice in business matters that he will assume to act on her behalf without previous consultation, but this does not mean that he has reserved legal power to do so when making her the gift.

Apart from wondering how the last sentence of the previous paragraph would be received today, it is probably sensible to skip the further explanation of the Judge's rationale for finding in Wodehouse's favour, pausing only to note that the dissenting Judge Clark would

> ... at the very least, return the case for fuller trial [to permit the Wodehouses to appear and give evidence as to donative intent] ...

and that he justified his distaste for the decision, inter alia, in the following words:

> To let him escape taxation because the assignment was made before, rather than after, the assured sale of the novel [in which case all the Judges agreed that the assignment would have been ineffective] seems to me to rely on the kind of nice distinction which the Supreme Court has often told us is not to be permitted to inhibit the taxing power [although, interestingly, in the UK, this type of transaction would almost certainly be effective for tax purposes even today].

> Our decision seems to me to provide a very easy way around taxes from property, over which in the eyes of the world the taxpayer retains full control.

One point which should be made is that by 21 November, 1949, when the Second Circuit court hearing took place, the Wodehouses had been back in the US for two and a half years, so the dissenting judge's suggestion should have been easy to accommodate if it had had more general support.

But the Second Circuit judges were less kind in relation to the other issues, following the Supreme Court (as they were obliged to) in finding for the IRS in respect of point (a) and declining to take the responsibility for introducing commonsense into the allocation of income between the USA and Canada, in respect of point (b).

And now we approach the *pièce de résistance*. The Fourth Circuit Appeal Court, having been reversed by the Supreme Court on point (a), could not bring itself to agree with any other Court on anything. Perhaps it suffered from a fit of pique (or Peke, as PGW always spelt it), because, despite having (or maybe because it had) the benefit of the decisions in the Second Circuit on identical issues, it flexed its muscles and demonstrated its independence by making judgments which were diametrically opposed to those of the Second Circuit. So it found that the gift to Ethel (point (c)) was not effective for tax purposes, but agreed that part of the proceeds from the sale of serial rights should be allocated to Canada and thus be exempt from tax.

This extraordinary turn of events did not mean that the cases were finished. The Fourth Circuit disdained to dirty its fingers in making the actual allocation of revenue between the US and Canada, because this was a matter of fact for the lower court to find, and this was remitted back to the Tax Court, where the whole story began several years earlier, to undertake this task, on which it was to pronounce on 6 December, 1950.

Meanwhile, Wodehouse was keeping his friends up to date with developments, and gratuitous comments on the all-pervasive nature of tax and the tax authorities. In a letter to Townend dated 9 January, 1950, he indirectly exposed the lack of ethical principles of one income tax expert, whose professional creed should undoubtedly have been, "Never disclose a fact about one client to anybody else":

> Incidentally, I was lunching with John Golden the other day and Kelland's name came up and John said "How much do you think Clarence Buddington Kelland makes a year?" and I said "Well he probably gets $ 40,000 for a *Post* serial and doesn't seem to do much other work, so call it $ 50,000." Upon which John Golden told me that he had the same income tax expert as Kelland and the income tax expert had told him as an absolute fact that Kelland's income for 1949 was over $ 300,000!!!!

Towards the end of the year (30 October), he made observations on two points, one demonstrating the continued awareness of cash flow, and the other now seeming to approve of the $ 1,000 deduction for being a fallen angel. Note that, in the last sentence, he perpetuates the myth that a tax deduction means a dollar for dollar reduction in the tax bill:

> Did I tell you that Didier didn't pay me an advance on my last book, so I told him the contract was broken, and he is now hanging on to all the money he owes me — quite a large sum — and I am suing him. It's a great nuisance, but my lawyer tells me I am sure to win, and one comfort is that, if and when I get the money, it will come into my 1951 income tax and not 1950.

> Isn't it extraordinary that these plays [*Ring Around The Moon*] get produced over here, where it costs $ 60,000 to put the simplest play on. I think the solution is that, if you put $ 1,000 into a play and lose it, you can knock it off your income tax, so people with a bit of money to spare think they might just as well lose it in the theatre as give it to the Government.

And he was not above concern for the tax problems of others, as shown in a letter to Guy Bolton on 4 November, 1950:

> I am delighted that Prince Littler likes your adaptations so much. The only thing that worries me is, what are you doing about English income tax? Are they letting you pay American income tax in spite of being in England so long?

In due course the Tax Court convened to hear the case concerning Canadian sales, remitted to it from the Fourth Circuit Appeal Court. And true to form, we find it apparently overturning logic yet again. It decided that, whereas the *Saturday Evening Post* made about 4.3% of its North American sales in Canada compared to just 2.4% by the *Cosmopolitan*, there should nevertheless be an allocation to Canada of only 8.75% ($ 3,500) of each of the payments received from the *Post*, but 15% ($ 300) of the much smaller payment from *Cosmopolitan*!

Maybe there were good reasons; maybe this is merely an illustration of a phenomenon well-known in England, the proposition that in general lawyers only understand figures when they are either the page numbers of a document or the bottom line of a fee note. But it does, perhaps, represent a fitting finale to a sorry tale. Wodehouse's comments on tax to his friends did not stop; his characters increased their output as will be seen in what remains of this chapter and the next. But his trials and tribulations were over, and there is no record of him having further difficulties with the tax officials.

By any standards, his experiences were more than unfortunate. The accusation of fraud, serious in itself and particularly difficult to stomach for an innocent who believed himself, however erroneously, to be fully and competently advised by independent professionals, was arbitrary and unforgivable. The route by which the true technical points were taken through the Courts were in accordance with the established administrative procedures, but demonstrate just how unhappily those procedures can operate.

One must wonder at a system which permits the same point being decided differently on matters of law, by different courts of the same standing, the taxpayer effectively having to rely on pot luck as to whether the decision would be found in his favour or not. In this series of cases, the taxpayer ended up not knowing on which basis he should file future tax returns, or even whether he needed to correct tax returns for the intervening periods — because this would depend on where he was physically resident and thus with which IRS office he was actually filing his returns!

We should not be surprised at Wodehouse's jaundiced view of tax

We should not be surprised at Wodehouse's jaundiced view of tax collectors; they in turn should thank their lucky stars that they got away so lightly at the hands of a victim so skilled in finding the telling phrase. And they did get away lightly. During the period covered by this chapter, perhaps showing the sensitivity lacking in his tormentors, he only mentioned tax in four publications. In **Spring Fever**[5], he wrote in his pre-war style, about the problems of the nobility in England:

> These times in which we live are not good times for earls. Theirs was a great racket while it lasted, but the boom days are over. A scattered few may have a pittance, but the majority, after they have paid their income tax and their land tax and all their other taxes and invested in one or two of the get-rich-quick schemes thrown together for their benefit by bright-eyed gentlemen in the City, are generally pretty close to the bread line. Lord Shortlands, with two and eightpence in his pocket, was more happily situated than most.

In **Uncle Dynamite**[6], he reverted in part to the plot of **The Luck of the Bodkins,** in which problems arose from the wish of a woman with personality to have a somewhat more timid gentleman smuggle jewellery through customs. Pongo Twistleton was complaining to Lord Ickenham when the topic was introduced:

> "... She was always trying to boss me."

> "Girls do. Especially American girls. I know, because I married one. It's part of their charm."

> "Well, there's a limit."

> "And with you that was reached — how? You had started to tell me. What was it she wanted you to do?"

> "Take some jewellery with me when I went to New York and smuggle it through the customs."

"Bless her heart, what an enterprising little soul she is. But since when has Sally possessed jewellery?"

"It wasn't for her, it was for one of her rich American pals, a girl named Alice something. This ass of a female had been loading herself up with the stuff in and around Bond Street and didn't like the idea of paying duty on it when she got back to New York, and Sally wanted me to run it through for her."

"A kindly thought."

"A fatheaded thought. And so I told her. A nice chump I should have looked, being disembowelled by port officials."

This problem led to a disagreement of substance between Pongo and Sally Painter, but Lord Ickenham took it upon himself to repair the damage:

"... And when I cursed him for being ass enough to part brass rags with you, he told me the inside story."

"About my wanting him to smuggle Alice Vansittart's jewels into America?"

"Yes."

"I was a fool to get mad. And it was all so unnecessary, as it turned out."

"The Vansittart decided on reflection to pay duty?"

"No, But I thought of a much better way of slipping the stuff through. I'm not going to tell even you what it was, but it's a peach of a way. It can't fail. Alice is crazy about it."

Clues to Lord Ickenham's idea can be gleaned from the following two extracts of his conversations with Sir Aylmer Bostock (an ex-Governor of Crown colonies and a tough egg), which appear during the *dénouement*.

> "... Well, when [Sally] had got them, the thought flashed upon her that on arriving with them in New York, she would have to pay heavy customs duty to the United States Government. She recoiled from this."
>
> "I don't blame her."
>
> "So in her innocent, girlish way she decided to smuggle them in."
>
> "Quite right. Don't pay the bounders a penny, that's what I say. They've got too much money as it is."

And a few exchanges of conversation later:

> ... She went to [a sculptress friend], got her to make a clay bust and put the jewels in its head, and was then all set to take them to America in safety and comfort. She reasoned that when the customs authorities saw a clay bust, they would simply yawn and say "Ho hum, a clay bust," and let it through.

The other reference to tax in this work could not have been more different, and demonstrates the breadth of Wodehouse's vision on this topic. Pongo has just had the threat that he would be required to judge a bonny babies competition transferred from his shoulders to those of Bill Oakshott. He had been part of a threesome with Sir Aylmer and Lady Bostock while the matter was discussed but had been left on his own after their departure.

> ... Pongo followed them.
>
> He felt he needed air. A similar sensation had often come to sensitive native chiefs at the conclusion of an

interview with Sir Aylmer Bostock on the subject of unpaid hut taxes.

Also in 1948, there was a passing reference to tax in the Wodehouse/Bolton collaboration which appeared under the name Stephen Powys, ie *Don't Listen, Ladies*[7]. Early in the play, Daniel was speaking to his wife, Madeleine:

> "I see? If your wife has a lover, you should accept it as one accepts bad weather or the income-tax? Minor misfortunes that only dull people talk about?"

An insight into Wodehouse's view of himself as dull, perhaps, bearing in mind the extensive correspondence on the subject with Townend and Bolton himself. Or was this sentence inserted by Guy Bolton as a little dig at Wodehouse? Whichever is the correct interpretation, it brings to mind a comment attributed to Evelyn Waugh by Frances Donaldson in *Evelyn Waugh: Portrait of a Country Neighbour*[8] but denied by Wodehouse himself, according to Barry Phelps in *P G Wodehouse — Man and Myth*[9]:

> ... a public luncheon was given for [Evelyn] by the editress of *Vogue*, who asked him whether there was any particular person he would like to have invited. He immediately named P G Wodehouse. His hostess replied that if he wished Mr Wodehouse to be asked he must invite him himself, and Evelyn went to some pains to do this. When he returned he told us that Plummy had come to the luncheon and been given the place of honour next to him.
>
> "Well...?" we asked.
>
> Evelyn gave his expostulatory chuckle.
>
> "It wasn't very amusing," he said, "I could not persuade him to talk on any subject except income tax."

The tale is reminiscent of one told by Wodehouse about Bernard Shaw in 1951 (see page 195). To the extent that the story contains any elements of truth, it is likely that the discussion was a two-way affair. Evelyn Waugh is also reported as being resentful at paying out large parts of his earnings to the State, and this burning sense of injustice may well have restricted his output as a writer. In later correspondence with Wodehouse the two rejoiced in a successful libel suit conducted by Evelyn Waugh against Nancy Spain, especially as sums of money earned in this way seemed to them to be about the only remaining source of tax-free receipt!

Wodehouse's final reference to tax in this period appeared in a Jeeves novel, **The Mating Season**[10], and were perhaps his best and most concise lines on the subject in the whole of his works. They form part of a conversation between Catsmeat Pirbright, the first speaker, and Bertie Wooster:

> "Why, dash it, if I could think of some way of doing down the income-tax people, I should be a rich man. You don't know a way of doing down the income-tax people, do you, Bertie?"

> "Sorry, no. I doubt if even Jeeves does."

Footnotes

1 47 BTA 691
2 *Saturday Evening Post, July 16, 1938 to September 3, 1938*
   Renamed **The Code of the Woosters** in book form. 1938, Herbert Jenkins
3 *Saturday Evening Post, April 22, 1939 to May 27, 1939* 1939,
   Herbert Jenkins
4 *Saturday Evening Post, May 4, 1940 to June 22, 1940* 1940, Herbert Jenkins
5 1948, Herbert Jenkins
6 1948, Herbert Jenkins
7 1948, Samuel French
8 1976, Weidenfeld & Nicholson
9 1992, Constable
10 1949, Herbert Jenkins

CHAPTER 8: 1951 to 1975 — CALMER WATERS

This chapter does not have any of the tension and excitement generated by a lunatic bureaucracy, and consists mainly of a series of references to taxes in almost thirty books and articles written after 1950. But a few pieces of relevant correspondence were spread evenly across the 1950s, and cover a variety of angles on the dreaded subject. The first, almost inevitably, appeared in a letter to Townend, dated 31 January, 1951:

> Bernard Shaw. Didn't it make you sick when you read about his will? With people starving on every side and doctors needing every penny they can get for cancer research and so on, he leaves his entire fortune to starting a new alphabet. I believe the man was dotty. I met a man who was with him a lot in his last days and all GBS would talk about was his income tax. You would feel that when you got to 94 and had a million or so salted away that you would feel it didn't matter much what the income tax authorities nipped you for.
>
> We see a lot of the Sax Rohmers. I like him but think his work is terrible. Mrs Rohmer is the sister of Knox of Nervo & Knox and she was telling us that Knox makes £ 700 a week and after taxes gets about £ 30 a week. Is this possible even in England? If so I should have thought it would pay him better to take £ 60 and have an arrangement with the management by which they would stand him lunch and dinner every day. Over here, though it is bad, it's much better than in England. I paid my income tax a week or so ago and it came to about a third of my income. In England they would have started by slicing off half of it.

He followed this up, on 22 April, with a plaintive cry about the iniquities of the idiom that possession is nine points of the law:

The more I see of Governments, the more I dislike them. In 1943 the US Government pinched $ 40,000 of mine, claiming that I had paid no tax in 1921 and various other things. I won two out of the three law suits and they owe me about $ 20,000 but it is months since the last case was decided and not a sign of them brassing up. Yet I had to pay a chunk of my 1952 income tax in advance. The only consolation is that they have to pay me 6% on the money back to 1943 so I suppose the longer they wait the better for me as you can't get more than 6% on an investment.

And he showed continued concern for his friends, first for Bill Townend on 15 April, 1952:

I am enclosing an ASCAP *[American Society of Composers, Authors and Playwrights]* cheque. I wish you would let me know if these get by all right and — particularly — whether you are paying income tax on them. Don't pay income tax, as I look after that over here. These cheques are gifts and you don't have to pay tax on them.

That advice was correct, and perhaps Wodehouse was preparing an alternative career for himself as a tax expert, because he later gave Guy Bolton very sound and proper warnings that he should double-check his UK tax position, when staying for a prolonged period and buying a house in the UK, in letters of 1 May, 1958, and 20 June, 1959:

What sensational news that you have bought a house! It sounds ideal. Are you sure about that taxation thing, that Americans can live permanently in England and only pay on what they earn in England? Because if so, you are on velvet. I suppose England really is the place to live, but we are getting more and more tied down to Remsenberg.

I am a bit uneasy about that flat you've taken and are renting. Doesn't ownership of a flat make you liable for English income tax? It's a thing you have to be very careful about. Consult a legal eagle, is my advice.

In a highly confused letter to Guy Bolton of 30 April, 1954, Wodehouse's total lack of understanding of matters of a technical financial nature was made plain. He fails to understand the difference between sales proceeds, on the one hand, and profit or loss, on the other. It is another example of the point made in the last chapter when he equated tax *reduction* with tax *deduction*:

Do you understand the financial mind? We have some investments which have gone up in value, and a financial expert has sold some which have gone down, so that the losses will wipe out the gains, thus saving us income tax. But, dash it, this must be looney. Suppose you make a profit on a stock of $ 1,000. Right. The Government want 50%. Alright, you pay them their 50% and still, unless I am cuckoo, have another $ 500 in the sock. But if you make a profit of $ 1,000 and then immediately sell something which gives you a loss of $ 1,000, it seems to me that you are $ 500 to the bad or, if not $ 500, at any rate something. Oh well.

On 7 October, he wrote to Bill Townend with some comments on his taking American citizenship, which is **not** done purely for tax purposes! But tax does come into it:

I have been swamped with correspondence, mainly about my taking American Citizenship. All the letters have been very friendly.

I don't know that I would have done it if Ethel had not urged me to. But I think it's a good move. So far from keeping me out of England, it will improve the situation a lot. Till now I have always had the idea that there might be trouble if I went to England (because of the judge's decision about the broadcasts) but I imagine they would hardly dare to arrest an American Citizen! And there are all sorts of minor advantages, eg that if you leave the States you don't have to have an exit and a re-entrance permit and you don't have to pay all your income tax up to the date when you sail.

But since he never left the US again, Wodehouse was not to benefit from those advantages.

The final piece of correspondence was a brief letter to Guy Bolton, dated 7 April, 1958. In a way, it is rather fitting, because it contains an implication that he followed a very minor course of action simply because by doing so he would receive a tax deduction. In the context of the subject-matter that can hardly be correct, but the phraseology does suggest it, and it reaffirms the point that tax was rarely out of Wodehouse's thoughts:

> I enclose a letter from Watty. Wattenburg must be cuckoo. When in the last 40 years have I had my lyrics in any picture? Surely, except for *Bill*, only in the Jerome Kern Life[1], and then we got a straight £ 1,000 per lyric, didn't we? Harms never cut themselves in on that, did they? I told Watty about the J K Life and he said you had already told him. He tells me we can deduct all legal expenses from income tax, so I told him to go ahead.

* * * * *

Tax and tax collectors were very much more to the fore in his writings after the Court cases were settled. In **The Old Reliable**[2], four references were dotted about, starting with a conversation between Bill Shannon, the first speaker, and Joe Davenport concerning the need Bill had for twenty thousand dollars to set up a literary agency:

"... Aren't you putrescent with money?"

"I've a thousand dollars if you call that putrescent."

"A thousand? What's become of that radio jackpot?"

"Gone with the wind."

"You dissolute young rat."

"High cost of living, taxes and so on ... "

But all was not lost, or at least, it did not appear to be lost, when Joe bumped into a large, stout, elderly gentleman who looked like a Roman Emperor who has been doing himself too well on the starchy foods:

> For to Joe, meeting him here, it was obvious who this was. It could be none other than the plutocrat Cork, the super-tax-paying mate of Kay's Aunt Adela.

Bill Shannon, sister of Adela, discovered that her English butler, Phipps, was a trained safe-breaker, and pondered on the ethics of not informing her sister, because:

> The generosity of the late Albert Cork, combined with her personal and private fortune, the outcome of pulling down a huge salary in the days before there was any income tax to speak of, had left Adela with sufficient jewellery to equip half the blondes in Hollywood ...

As in all Wodehouse books misunderstandings abound, one of which occurred in chapter 18, when Bill was discussing with Lord Topham the financing of a potentially very successful authors' representation business:

[Lord Topham speaks first]

199

"You'll make a fortune."

"Exactly. The same thought occurred to me. We shall have to spend the rest of our lives thinking up ways of doing down the income tax authorities ..."

Taxation could not have been prevented from appearing in the Blandings series. In **Pigs Have Wings**[3], the need for professional advice is paramount, first when the Earl of Emsworth was discussing Penelope Donaldson with his sister Constance:

"What's she going to London for in weather like this? Silly idea."

"She has a fitting. Her dress for the County Ball. And Orlo has to see his lawyer about his income tax."

"Income tax!" cried Lord Emsworth, starting like a war horse at the sound of a bugle. Pigs and income tax were the only two subjects that really stirred him. "Let me tell you — "

"I haven't time to listen," said Lady Constance, and swept away from the room.

and later, when Gally's conversation with Orlo Vosper is interrupted by an announcement that Mr Wapshott has arrived for an appointment with Orlo, Gally shows his usual interest in the affairs of others:

"Who is this Wapshott?"

"My income tax chap," said Lord Vosper. "Fellow who looks after my income tax," he added, clarifying the situation still further.

And when a penniless suitor is giving the rundown on his financial position, the reply must, of course, take tax payments into account:

Jerry [Vail] laughed bitterly.

"Let me supply you with a few statistics relating to my financial position," he said. "My income last year, after taxes, was — "

In his book **Lord Emsworth's Annotated Whiffle**[4], James Hogg picked up the peer's antipathy to income tax. On page 107, the text reads:

Seekers after sensation will go to great lengths to dress up a meat which in my view needs no improvement. The Romans are said to have fed their pigs on dried figs and honeyed wine to enrich the flavour (apart from being unnecessary it would not be an economic proposition today, with the iniquitous burden of tax borne by the propertied class).

The annotation by Lord Emsworth in the margin reads:-

Whiffle absolutely right about this.

The English and American peoples are said to be a single race divided by a common language, but that the dislike of taxes is a common failing easily understood by both groups was illustrated by a conversation between the American actor Mervyn Potter and the ultra-English Barmy Fotheringay-Phipps (pronounced Fungy-Fipps), in **Barmy in Wonderland**[5]:

"I'll tell you what I'd do, if I were as rich as you."

This surprised Barmy.

"Aren't you?"

"Of course I'm not. We Hollywood hams are not rich men, Phipps. We think we are for a few happy moments when we are counting the contents of the envelope on pay day, and then we feel a tap on our shoulder; there, standing beside us waiting to twist our arm, is a gentleman with whiskers who takes it all off us, skinning us to the bone."

"Taxes, you mean?"

Mervyn Potter winced.

"Don't mention that word, Phipps. Without wishing to wound, you have touched an exposed nerve. Yes, taxes, if you must have it."

"I suppose they're pretty big."

"Supercolossal........."

Evident wealth remained in Wodehouseland, an indication that tax bills would be high, and high tax bills meant that the tax authorities would not be far behind. So in **Ring For Jeeves**[6], when it is necessary to describe Mrs Spottsworth, her status is immediately recognised by a description of her tax-paying potential:

The thing about her that immediately arrested the attention and drew the startled whistle to the lips was the aura of wealth which she exuded. It showed itself in her rings, her hat, her stockings, her shoes, her platinum fur cape and the Jacques Fath sports costume that clung lovingly to her undulating figure. Here, you would have said to yourself, beholding her, was a woman who had got the stuff in sackfuls and probably suffered agonies from coupon-clipper's thumb, a

woman at the mention of whose name the blood-
sucking leeches of the Internal Revenue Department
were accustomed to raise their filthy hats with a
reverent intake of breath.

Mild abuse, but nonetheless descriptive of Wodehouse's opinion
of those who had caused him so much trouble. The next year, in
Jeeves and the Feudal Spirit[7], he reverts to the traditional views
of Bertie's Uncle Tom Travers:

Uncle Tom, though abundantly provided with the chips,
having been until his retirement one of those merchant
princes who scoop it up in sackfuls out East, has a
rooted objection to letting the hell hounds of the Inland
Revenue dip in and get theirs. For weeks after they
have separated him from his hard-earned he is inclined
to go off into corners and sit with his head in his hands,
muttering about ruin and the sinister trend of socialistic
legislation and what is to become of us all if this
continues.

And later Bertie has an interview with his uncle in which the same
topic is raised:

He then spoke with considerable fervour for a while of
income-tax and surtax, and after making a tentative
appointment to meet me in the breadline at an early
date, popped off and was lost in the night.

When Jeeves requests leave to attend a luncheon at the Junior
Ganymede to say farewell to a member who is accompanying the
new British Ambassador to the US, Bertie happily agrees,
approving of the approach adopted by the said ambassador, in
particular the fact that he is moving to the US:

"One likes to see these public servants bustling about
and earning their salaries."

"Yes, sir."

203

"If one is a taxpayer, I mean, contributing one's whack to those salaries."

Many of Wodehouse's minor articles, quips or anecdotes in this period appeared in **Punch**, and no less than 20 references to tax appear in those articles. This demonstrates that the subject was always to the forefront of his mind, especially when preparing minor pieces of writing, such as articles and essays.

It is probably convenient to include all these pieces together with little commentary, although it is ironic that the first reference which appeared was actually a parody by J MacLaren Ross entitled "**Good Lord, Jeeves**[8]".

> *[Jeeves has been given a Cabinet Post, the Drones Club of which Wooster is now secretary has been requisitioned by the Ministry of Rehabilitation, and Wooster is concerned for his job]*
>
> "... But you were saying about your position as secretary here, and its importance to you ... "
>
> "Supreme importance, Jeeves, financially speaking. Nationalization and super-tax have taken their toll. The Wooster millions are, in fact, down the drain. Need I say more?"

Readers will be pleased to hear that Jeeves offered Wooster a job as his personal attendant, enabling him to take the vacancy as secretary at the Junior Ganymede Club.

The other contributions to **Punch** were:

30 June, 1954   *Bring Back that Cuculus*

This was essentially the source of the essay in the first item described below relating to **America I Like You**[9]/**Over Seventy**[10].

29 September, 1954   *Carol and Edna*

Again, essentially the source of the essay on hurricanes referred to below, in **Over Seventy**.

16 February, 1955   *Onwards and Upwards With the Fiends*

But my chief complaint against these fiends is that they don't know how to spend their money. The way I look at it is, it's no good sitting motionless like a spider in the centre of its web and having your agents rob banks and steal jewels and secret treaties — which is where the big profit is these days. No income tax — if you don't get anything out of it ... What does Professor Moriarty do? If he isn't working out problems on a blackboard in Pinner (or some similar suburb, for Holmes speaks of "ten miles away") you will find him in an underground gas chamber in Stepney. That's no way to live.

18 May, 1955   *Thoughts on the Crime Wave*

... I find myself wondering why it is worth these crime wavers' while to take so much trouble for such small results.

I am not, of course, speaking of the swells who rob banks and loot the apartments of Texas millionaires. They make a nice living, their earnings being substantial and free of tax.

13 July, 1955   *Attention, All Patrons*

... It would be a start towards reviving the old Patron system, the lapse of which we authors have all regretted so much. Let the slogan be *Back to the Eighteenth Century.*

Those were the days. None of that modern nonsense then of the young writer submitting his novel to the scrutiny of a beady-eyed publisher and having to listen to him talking about the growing cost of paper and the impossibility under existing conditions of springing the smallest advance. All you had to do was to run over the roster of the peerage and select your man. You wanted somebody pretty weak in the head, but practically all members of the peerage in those happy times were weak in the head and, there being no income tax or supertax, they had the stuff in sackfuls.

28 December, 1955   *World's Workers*

... the man one really admires is Charles Wenzel of Hoboken, because he did down the income-tax authorities.

Income tax was inaugurated in the United States in 1913. No doubt it seemed to the authorities a good idea at the time, but most people feel that it was a mistake to allow it to develop into such a popular craze. Charles Wenzel was more courageous than most of us, and he decided to do something about it. He was recently accused of having received seven income tax refunds totalling $ 2,500, and evidence was brought to show that he was waiting for seventeen more government cheques averaging $ 400 each.

Apparently his mode of procedure was to file a bogus return under a false name but a correct address, and then wait for the refund which he claimed. An unmarried man, he gave himself a wife and five children, and was just saying to himself "Nice going, Charlie. 'At's the stuff to give 'em, Wenzel," when Raymond Del Tufto Jr, United States attorney for New Jersey, came down on him like a ton of bricks.

8 February, 1956   *Basso Profundo*

Merely refers back to **Thoughts on the Income Tax** from **Louder and Funnier**.

17 April, 1957   *America Day by Day*

Over here at the moment we are all very interested in the financial affairs of Joe Louis. When in the ring in his capacity of heavyweight champion of the world, Joe earned $ 4,626,721, which is admittedly nice money, and the Internal Revenue authorities have suddenly woken up to the fact that he owes them about two million of the best and brightest. It appears that the lawyers and accountants to whom he had entrusted the payment of income tax let their minds wander and forgot all about it.

17 July, 1957   *America Day by Day*

Leonard F Genz of Greenwich, Conn., is a man who can be pushed just so far. When they upped his Federal and State taxes, as they are doing all the time these days, he did not wince nor cry aloud but wrote a cheque and posted it to the local vampire bats. But when he got a New York State tax form which included the words "Give complete address used for 1956 if different than the above" he felt the time had come to make a stand. He wrote to Governor Harriman about it. I don't know what he said, but it was probably something not very different than "Well, youse guys up in Albany certainly laid an egg that time. Ain't you never been to school and been learned grammar? Where do you get that different than stuff? Different *from*, you poor uneducated slobs."

207

The point, in the opinion of most taxpayers, is well taken. What I mean to say, ginks like I and you and the rest of us don't mind having our blood sucked annually by a bunch of Draculas, but we think they got a nerve when they suck it like as if they'd never of heard of any such a bozo as Fowler, if you see what I mean.

12 March, 1958　　　*America Day by Day*

To one who, like myself, is fond of Governments, and particularly that branch of them that handles income tax, it has come as a nasty blow to learn that the Director of Internal Revenue has lost his ten-year battle with Mr Louis F Williams of 219 Clinton Street, Brooklyn, over that business of the $ 2,528.51. US District Judge Robert A Inch has ruled that the Statute of Limitations precludes the Director from getting back a cent of it.

In case you have not been following the thing, what happened was that in 1948 Mr Williams claimed a refund of the sum I have mentioned, and it was only after he had trousered it and spent it that the authorities found that he was not entitled to it. One can imagine their feelings. Picture Dracula suddenly discovering that he had inadvertently overlooked a pint of blood, and you will have the idea. For the next ten years they wrote Mr Williams what my morning journal describes as "a long series of unconvincing letters" with a view to inducing him to part, and now it is too late.

It would be interesting to read this correspondence. I imagine it started with a lot of that "Sir, This is to inform you that unless you immediately————" stuff, and became more and more plaintive over the years till finally it got down to "Listen, old man ... " and "Ah, come on, Louis, be a sport."

Talking of Louis and income tax, you may recall that Joe Louis was behind-hand with his to the tune of, if I remember correctly, about two million bucks. He has now made an arrangement with the authorities to pay them so much a year till his obligations are fulfilled, and should be all square by 2018 or 2020 at the latest. Nice going, Joe.

20 May, 1959   *Baker St W1   From a Detective's Notebook*

(The story in which Adrian Mulliner proves conclusively that Professor Moriarty was actually Sherlock Holmes.)

"... Why is a man casual about money?"

"Because he has a lot of it."

"Precisely."

"But you said Holmes hadn't."

"I said nothing of the sort. That was merely the illusion he was trying to create."

"Why?"

"Because he needed a front for his true activities. Sherlock Holmes had no need to worry about fees. He was pulling in the stuff in sackfuls from another source. Where is the big money? Where has it always been? In crime. Bags of it, and no income tax. If you want to salt away a few million for a rainy day you don't spring into 9.30 trains to go and see governesses, you become a master criminal, sitting like a spider in the centre of its web and egging on your corps of assistants to steal jewels and naval treaties."

A little self-derivative, as usual for this sort of piece.

Over here in these United States the man we all proudly greet at the moment is Raymond B Umbaugh (pronounced, say sources close to him, like the sort of toot you get when you blow on a tuba), who has just come out with the Umbaugh Plan for "ever-mounting productivity to the golden age of private capital". This may seem a little vague to the lay mind, but the next words in the manifesto aren't, for he says he is going to get rid of personal income tax by 1963.

I was speaking in my last communiqué of Mr Raymond B Umbaugh and his plan for doing away with income tax, and I think I made it clear that most red-blooded Americans are all for it and wish him the best of luck. There is, however, one section of the community that takes only an academic interest in the Umbaugh Plan — the Mohawk Tribe of Indians, who claim that as a sovereign state they are immune from taxation and say they are blowed if they are going to let the Government have so much as a nickel from the old oak chest. Their hereditary chief Alex Gray — surely this is a misprint for Flying Cloud or Bounding Beaver or something like that — has issued a statement to the press that any official entering the reservation to collect income tax from brave or squaw will be treated as a burglar. And we all know how Red Indians treat burglars. The unhappy slobs get scalped before they can say What ho.

Little wonder that Robert Clark, who runs the local tax office, informs us that "attempts at direct collection have failed". All American income tax collectors have lovely heads of hair, and they have no wish to jeopardize them.

Until recently one had always thought of Los Angeles as a city where you could have a pretty good time if you didn't mind being choked by the smog, but now it seems that there are any number of disadvantages to living there. The men up top, anxious to scoop in enough doubloons to balance the budget, are slapping a weight tax on all citizens who, neglecting to watch their calories, send the scales up to over fourteen stone four, a $ 1,000-a-year impost on the unmarried, and of all things for sunny California a bathing suit tax.

You can offer a termite the finest fillet steak or a perfectly prepared *Timbale de ris de veau Toulousane* and it will turn its head away and stick to wood, and this has caused mental anguish to thousands, for until recently it was not permissible to deduct termite damage from income tax.

"Termites," the authorities argued, "do not constitute casualty losses—that is to say, destruction of property of a sudden and unexpected nature," and the taxpayers retorted that if there was anything more sudden and unexpected than the abrupt emergence of a bunch of beastly ants with their mouths full of desirable suburban villa they had yet to hear of it.

It is pleasant to be able to report that the Bureau of Internal Revenue has at last seen the light, and as of even date, if the ceiling falls down on you accompanied by a shower of termites chewing busily and telling one another that there is nothing like a bit of wood for breakfast, you can chalk it up on the credit side when making out your annual return.

17 August, 1960   *Our Man in America*

Well, sir, there was this shoe store out Detroit way, and
the oftener George Bottlinger thought to himself that if
only he could tie up the manager and the three
assistants and put them in a back room, he could make
a bit of non-taxable money, because anyone could see
the place was doing a thriving business.

11 January, 1961   *Our Man in America*

Disaffection is raising its ugly head in New York, and it
is not too much to say that there is a good deal of
sullen murmuring going on.

It's about those Gracie House meat and grocery bills.
We poor slobs of taxpayers have to pick up the check
for all the food consumed at Gracie House, the beautiful
residence on the East River where the Mayor of New
York lives with his wife and his two growing boys, and
as some of us are pretty strapped for money these
days, it is not surprising that the news that their bills for
what A P H calls obesity-producing carbohydrates are
averaging three thousand dollars a month has hit us
hard. A bit high, we feel.

24 May, 1961   *Our Man in America*

President Kennedy has been suggesting to Congress
that the fellows who make deductions in their income
tax returns for "legitimate business expenses" should
draw the line somewhere, and what has stunned the
citizenry is the discovery that all this time the income
tax authorities had hearts of gold. We have been
getting them all wrong. No Scrooges they, as *Time*
would say. In fact, slap a white beard on him and give
him a red robe and some stomach padding, and the
average income tax inspector could double as Santa
Claus, and no questions asked.

For years apparently these kindly souls have been allowing almost everyone to charge almost everything. Take the case of the undertaking firm and its yachting parties. What do undertakers want with a yacht, you ask. Perfectly simple. They "ship bodies to other areas for burial", and for that of course they need a yacht. And as my daily paper says, one doesn't just sit around and wait for such business to turn up. One goes after it by entertaining people whose recommendations to clients would be valuable, and how more suitably than on a yacht trip? A sympathetic Government allowed these seagoing undertakers to deduct $ 35,000 over a three-year period, and another yachtsman to write off $ 16,943 because he needed the vessel in order to demonstrate to customers the value of shoes with non-stick soles.

Then there was the travelling insurance man who in 1957 claimed as deductions for meals, lodging, transportation, entertainment, etc., $ 135,000. "Oh, I say, old chap," the Government said, raising its eyebrows a little, "isn't that a bit thick? If you'd see your way to settle for $ 97,500..." "Well, if you insist," said the insurance man, but he was heard to mutter "Bloodsuckers! Bloodsuckers!" under his breath.

What makes me sore is the thought of all the stuff I have been giving away to the lads up Washington way all this time, when I might have been knocking off princely sums for "loss of literary income owing to dachshund jumping on back of neck at crucial point in novel, thereby causing taxpayer to forget excellent epigram just about to write".

21 February, 1962   *Our Man in America*

This piece was a fore-runner to the entry (see below) in **Cavalier** for April 1965 entitled **A Cool Look at Snails.**

If you notice a certain strain and touch of stiffness in the atmosphere when US Tax Commissioner Mortimer M Caplin meets a business man, it is due to the former's ruling that "A business meal may be deducted from income tax only if it takes place in a locale free from substantial distractions", for this has caused quite a good deal of heart burning in financial circles.

As Mr Bob Considine points out in the N Y Journal American, Mr Caplin is aiming at the business man who tries to write off a paper hat and one of those things that squeak, not to mention six courses with wine, when he was entertaining a prospect at the Hotsy Totsy Club — twenty-six can-can girls — and to a certain extent he may be right. Twenty-six can-can girls are a substantial distraction. But what if the businessman goes elsewhere where it is quieter and finds distractions there? At Bleeck's, where the newspapermen go for their refreshment, you find as a rule nothing more distracting than the match game and — toward the end of the day — possibly some singing of Sweet Adeline in close harmony, but someone not long ago rode a police horse into the bar, probably just when a dozen diners were preparing to write the cost of their meal off on the ground that it had taken place in a locale free from distractions. It would be interesting to know if their claims got by Mr Caplin.

That completes the survey from **Punch**, and it is clear that tax-related stories formed the basis of a remarkably high proportion of his anecdotes and mini-essays. His experiences had certainly not been forgotten!

It was about this time that Ira Gershwin again produced lyrics in which taxation was featured. In the 1953 show **Give A Girl A Break** the song *In Our United State* contained the following:

Our annual budget?
I'll let you judge it -
You do what you will with what's in our treasury
I won't investigate in our united state.

This is my platform:
That face and that form!
You will find that that's a permanent policy
Slated for our united state.

But there will be changes I'm unfolding:
Withholding taxes are through -
For when its you, dear, that I'm holding,
You can't withhold on me -
I can't withhold on you.

And in *A Star Is Born*, in 1954, the refrain of the song *Lose That Long Face* proclaims the failure of governments to levy a tax on a smile:

Go lose that long face, that long face -
Go 'long and get that long face lost.
The blues black out when they can see
A smile that says, "Move on. No vacancy!"
This panacea idea
I'm handing you without any cost.
There isn't any tax on it,
So just relax on it -
If you want trouble double-crossed.
Don't give into a frown;
Turn that frown upside-down,
And get yourself that long face lost!

The book which Wodehouse published in the US as **America, I Like You**[9], and in the UK, with variations, as **Over Seventy**[10] included a number of articles, essays and other short pieces which stood up by themselves, and as will be seen, were derived from short pieces in *Punch*. Several have references, minor or major, to tax, in a number of different contexts. For example in the context of an essay on letters to the press, drawing attention to the English habit of using pseudonyms to write complaining letters to the press:

215

I inadvertantly caused something of a flutter in the club, I remember, soon after I had taken silk, and got hauled over the coals by that splendid veteran Mother of Six (Oswaldtwistle).

"Gussie," he said to me one morning — I was writing under the name of Disgusted Taxpayer in those days, "I have a bone to pick with you ..."

That extract was derived from **America, I Like You**, but the equivalent essay in the English version expressed it slightly differently:

That, I fancy, is how Ruat Coelum and the others would have done it, but the letter which I have quoted is evidently the work of a beginner. Notice how he plunges at his subject like a man charging into a railway station refreshment-room for a gin and tonic five minutes before his train leaves. Old hands like Verb Sap and Indignant Taxpayer would have begun:

Sir,

My attention has been drawn ...

And of course, other examples appear in the context of whether crime pays. In the US version:

I bought the [gadget designed to baffle the criminal classes], and as I attached it to the door I found myself wondering why it is worth these crimewavers' while to take so much trouble for such small results.

I am not, of course, speaking of the aristocracy of the profession who rob banks and loot the apartments of Texas millionaires. They make a nice living, their earnings being substantial and free from income tax.

He was more explicit in the equivalent essay in **Over Seventy**, making that point and another:

> The prudent thing for anyone who wishes to provide for his old age is to find some steady job which will enable him to put by a certain something each week, so that every little bit added to what he has got makes just a little bit more, and one immediately thinks of crime, with its negligible overhead and freedom from income tax, as the solution.

> But while one respects practitioners like these and wishes them every success in their chosen careers, the world's worker one really admires is Robert Watson (45) of Hoboken, NJ, because he did down the income tax authorities — the dream of every red-blooded man. He was recently convicted of having received seven illegitimate tax refunds totalling $ 2,500, and evidence was brought to show he was waiting for seventeen more government cheques averaging $ 400 each.

A remarkable coincidence, don't you think, that Charles Wenzel (who appeared in **Punch**) also came from Hoboken!

When collecting material for **America, I Like You**, Wodehouse evidently realised that his collection of essays entitled **Louder and Funnier**[11] had not been published in the **US**. The original essay on which **Thoughts on the Income Tax** (which appeared in **Louder and Funnier**) was based had originally appeared in **Vanity Fair** in 1919, before undergoing significant expansion and revision. But the longer version of the essay had not been exposed to the US public, and as always, ever prepared to recycle good material, he included yet another version in **America, I Like You** under the title **Blessings in Disguise**:

"Well, from what you have been telling us, Mr Wodehouse, it would seem that you have quite a high opinion of this America of ours."

"Extremely high. The land of the free and the home of the brave, I sometimes call it."

"Any criticisms?"

"One or two, perhaps."

"Let's have them."

"You won't be offended?"

"No, no. Go right ahead."

"Well, take, for instance, income tax."

"You view it with concern?"

"Of the deepest description."

"How well I know that feeling. There was no income tax when you first came over here, was there?"

"No. They started it in 1913. No doubt it seemed to the authorities a good idea at the time, but I think they have overdone it. It was a mistake to allow it to develop into such a popular craze. And the whole spirit has changed since those early days."

"In what way?"

"Well, take the case of a friend of mine back in 1914. He found, on going over his income tax return, that he had overpaid the Internal Revenue the sum of $ 1.50. He wrote a civil letter, asking for a refund, and received an equally civil reply, in which the Internal Revenue regretted the error and begged to enclose, as requested, a check for $ 15. My friend returned the check, saying there had been a mistake, and the authorities, more apologetic than ever, sent him another for $ 150. When he returned this check, they almost grovelled and enclosed one for $ 1,500. My friend was content at this point to take his profit and retire from the game, but I still think that if he had had the vision and enterprise to carry on he could have cleaned them out. You wouldn't get anything like that happening nowadays."

"You certainly wouldn't. Of all the hard-boiled, stony-eyed, protruding-chinned lineal descendants of Jesse James who ever took the widow and the orphan by the scruff of the neck and rubbed their noses in the mud, these modern Internal Revenue thugs are the ... But I must not allow myself to become bitter. After all, there is a bright side to the income tax."

"I have not detected it myself."

"Well, look. Say what you will, the filling up of the forms has given us all a delightful indoor game in which young and old can take part with equal enjoyment. See the family clustered around the table. There is Father, with his spectacles on, jotting down some notes on Amortization. There is Mother, leaning over his shoulder and pointing out that by taking Sec. 6248H and putting it on top of Sub-sec. 9730G he can claim immunity from the tax mentioned in Sec. 4537M. And gathered about them are the children, sucking pencils and working out ways of doing down the supertax. You get the picture?"

"It rises before my eyes. "See, Papa," cries little Cyril gleefully, "I note that gifts (not made as a consideration for services rendered) and money and property acquired under a will or inheritance (but the income derived from money or property received by gift, will or inheritance) are, according to sub-sec. 2427, not subject to tax, and the way it looks to me is that you can knock off the price of the budgerigar's birdseed." And so it goes on, each helping the other, all working together in that perfect harmony which goes to make the happy home. Nor is this all."

"I know what you are going to say. Filling in the income tax forms has kindled again all the old spirit of love and family affection. How differently nowadays the head of the house regards his wife and children. Many a man who has spent years wondering why on earth he ever linked his lot with a woman whom he has disliked from the moment they entered the Niagara Falls Hotel and a gang of boys and girls who seemed to grow more repulsive every day gratefully revises his views as he scans Schedule C. His wife may be a nuisance about the home, but she enables him to split the income. And the children. As the father looks at their hideous faces and reflects that he is entitled to knock off a nice little sum per gargoyle, the austerity of his demeanor softens and he pats them on the head and talks vaguely about ice cream for supper."

"Profoundly true. I think I must withdraw my criticism of the income tax."

"I thought you would."

But it doesn't really seem that he meant it! The essay summarises, in the paragraph referring to Jesse James, Wodehouse's innermost thoughts about the IRS, and he was not shy in saying so.

Because of its appearance in **Louder and Funnier**, there was no equivalent essay in **Over Seventy**, the only similar item being a passing remark in an essay on changes which have occurred during the **75** years of Wodehouse's life:

What other changes? Well, there is the income tax. Am I wrong, or isn't it a bit stiffer than it used to be? I seem to remember a time when, if one sold a story, one spent most of the proceeds on a slap-up dinner somewhere, but now it never seems to run to much more than a ham sandwich. I suppose income tax is necessary, but I feel it was a mistake to allow it to develop into such a popular craze.

Over Seventy did include a number of other relevant essays, such as this example, on the decline of the patronage system for budding writers, cf the **Punch** article: **Attention All Patrons**:

You wanted somebody fairly weak in the head, but practically all members of the peerage in those days were weak in the head and, there being no income tax or super tax then, they could fling you purses of gold without feeling it. Probably some kindly friend put you on to the right man.

And this, on hurricanes:

The great thing to do when a hurricane comes clumping along and breaking all the trees in your garden — "Can we knock this off our income tax?" are the words you heard on every side in those days — is to look for the silver lining and try to spot the good it has wrought as well as the bad.

And finally from this source, tax featured in the poem **The Story of Otis**, previously published in **Punch** (September 9, 1956):

He clutched his head. "This is," he said, "the darndest thing I ever knew.
  I'd hoped for stacks of income tax to give the Internal Revenue,
    But now it seems those golden dreams, so roseate and fair withal,
Have got the axe. You can't pay tax if you haven't got the wherewithal."

221

But back to the novels. In **French Leave**[12], we find Terry Trent talking to Russell Clutterbuck about a forthcoming lunch.

> "This is not the true Russell Clutterbuck speaking," she said. "I can see what's the matter with you, my poor lamb. Subconsciously, without knowing it, you want your lunch. The trouble with you, Russ, is that you're so spiritual, you don't realize that you have to eat. Left to yourself, you would just sit here sniffing a rose and thinking beautiful thoughts. Where are you taking me? Make it somewhere good. You can knock it off your income tax under the head of Entertainment."

A highly practical suggestion, if true. But not likely to have been strictly in accordance with the rules. You normally have to be doing some business to knock the expense off your income tax.

In 1948, the post-war tax situation was so dire in the UK that excess profits tax at a rate of 100% could eliminate literally the whole of any incremental profits that a business might make in excess of those of the previous year. There is an apocryphal story of the three businessmen meeting for lunch, discussing business, but then arguing who was to pick up the bill.

> "Let me," said the first, adding with swelling chest, "I'm paying income tax at nineteen and six (97.5%) in the pound, so it will only cost me a tiny amount."

> "I'll pick it up," replied the second. "I'm paying excess profits tax at 100%, so it won't cost me a penny."

> "No," said the third. "I insist on paying it. I'm on a cost plus contract with the Government!"

After that digression, and returning to French Leave, there was a scene between Terry and old Nick, with Terry speaking:

> "Everyone seems to think he's going to make a fortune out of it."

The gleam in Old Nick's eye became more pronounced. A head waiter makes good money, but he can always do with a devoted son who pays surtax.

It wasn't only the National tax collectors that came in for the treatment. In **Something Fishy**[13], he commented in passing on the status of local tax gatherers:

> It was worth the sun's while to take a little trouble over Valley Fields, for there are few more pleasant spots on the outskirts of England's metropolis. One of its residents, a Major Flood-Smith, in the course of a letter to the **South London Argus** exposing the hellhounds of the local Rates and Taxes Department, once alluded to it as "a fragrant oasis".

When describing the wealth of one of the characters in the book, as in the case of the income of Jerry Vail (see page 201), it is of course essential to make clear that the level of an inheritance was after death duties. In this extract, Keggs is talking to Jane:

> "I make something of a hobby of following the sentimental ventures of the sons of Mr Bunyan's friends. Sentiment, I suppose."

> "Does you credit. Bunyan? Any relation of the Roscoe Bunyan who's taken Shipley?"

> "His father, miss. A very wealthy gentleman. Like so many others, he lost a great deal of money in the market crash of 1929, but I believe the younger Mr Bunyan inherited a matter of twenty million dollars after paying death duties."

By this time short stories about Jeeves and Bertie Wooster were somewhat rare, but in **Jeeves Makes an Omelette**[14] there was not only a short story but a reference back to what can instantly be recognised as Uncle Tom's undiluted and unchanged views:

Her [Aunt Dahlia's] allusion was to my uncle, Thomas Portarlington Travers, who foots the bills for what he always calls *Madame's Nightshirt*. He is as rich as creosote, as I believe the phrase is, but like so many of our wealthier citizens he hates to give up. Until you have heard Uncle Tom on the subject of income tax and supertax, you haven't heard anything.

And something very similar in 1960 when, at the start of **Jeeves in the Offing**[15], Aunt Dahlia is talking to Bertie on the telephone about the inmates at Brinkley Court, and has mentioned that Tom Travers has accompanied Homer Cream to Harrogate while he, Homer, takes the waters. But there is also a more positive note, the prospect of doing the enemy down!

"... Tom's in the middle of a very important business deal with Cream. If it goes through, he'll make a packet free of income tax. So he's sucking up to him like a Hollywood Yes-man."

I gave an intelligent nod, though this of course was wasted on her because she couldn't see me. I could readily understand my uncle-by-marriage's mental processes. T. Portarlington Travers is a man who has accumulated the pieces of eight in sackfuls, but he is always more than willing to shove a bit extra away behind the brick in the fireplace, feeling — and rightly — that every little bit added to what you've got makes just a little bit more. And if there's one thing that's right up his street, it is not paying income tax. He grudges every penny the Government nicks him for.

By the time of **Ice in the Bedroom**[16], as with the earlier **Pigs Have Wings**, the need for professional advisers was uppermost in his mind. The solicitor, Mr Shoesmith, who was adviser to Lord Blicester, was having a series of interruptions:

A wholesome awe of Leila Yorke, bred in him from the days of his youth, had kept [Mr Shoesmith] from throwing the girl out on her ear, as he had wished to do, but he had got rid of her as quickly as possible, and scarcely had she gone when his daughter Myrtle arrived, interrupting him at a moment when he had hoped to be free to attend to the tangled affairs of Freddie's uncle, Lord Blicester, who was having his annual trouble with the income tax authorities.

Wodehouse was aware of the addictive quality of tax problems, and happily injected Mr Shoesmith with a dose:

" ... " said Mr Shoesmith, trying not to speak petulantly but missing his objective by a wide margin. The conflict between Lord Blicester and the income tax authorities presented several points of nice legal interest, and he was longing to get back to them.

In the circumstances, it is not surprising that resolution of the technical problems took longer than Mr Shoesmith's client would have liked:

It was in no festive mood that [Lord Blicester] had come to Barribault's Hotel. Calling on Mr Shoesmith earlier in the morning to enquire how that income tax thing was working out ...

Wodehouse could never assume that his readers were old hands, and had to make sure that they were aware of all the personal prejudices of his characters. So once again, in **Stiff Upper Lip, Jeeves**[17], there is another reference to Uncle Tom's allergy in a conversation between Aunt Dahlia and Bertie:

"Tom's been feeling rather low of late because of what he calls iniquitous taxation. You know how he hates to give up."

I did, indeed. If Uncle Tom had his way, the Revenue authorities wouldn't get so much as a glimpse of his money.

"Well, I thought having to fraternize with Bassett would take his mind off it — show him there are worse things in the world than income tax. Our doctor here gave me the idea. He was telling me about a thing called Hodgkin's Disease that you cure by giving the patient arsenic. The principle's the same ... "

The Good Old Days were evidently those when tax rates, if positive, were in single or low double figures, and were recalled with affection or approval by Lord Tilbury in **Frozen Assets**[18]:

"He settled in America as a young man," said Lord Tilbury, becoming quite fluent, "and did extraordinarily well. Towards the end of his career he was one of New York's leading financiers, and as the greater part of his fortune was made before the days of high income taxes, he was at the time of his death extremely rich."

During 1964 and 1965, as a diversion, he built references to taxation into three articles, published in various magazines. The first was **Playboy** for January 1964, when in a piece entitled **Fox-hunting, Who Needs It?**, he put forward a theory as to the decline of the habit:

A variety of causes led to the sport's extinction. There have always been those who objected to it on humanitarian grounds, refusing to believe that the fox enjoyed the chase as much as anyone and feeling that with 60 hounds and a couple of hundred men with scarlet faces and women who looked like horses after it, it was not given a square deal.

226

But it was not these anti-bloodsport boys who killed the pastime. What did it was the high cost of the income tax. Maintaining a pack of hounds costs money, for these animals cannot give of their best unless they have square meals under their belts, and after two world wars money was just what the hunting community was short of. It was difficult enough to keep the home fires burning without going out of one's way to support a whole mob of canine pensioners.

In November 1964, in **Show**, he wrote an essay about black humour entitled **I don't get it...But then, I remember when humorists were funny**. In the introductory paragraph he elevates income tax to position of a senior depressant:

The French call it *humeur noir* in their quaint Gallic way. What the Germans and Italians and the Portuguese and the Argentines and the Greeks call it I don't know, but no doubt they call it something, for it has spread everywhere. I suppose the reason for its popularity is that, like the family in the famous Thurber drawings, everyone is disenchanted nowadays. What with income tax, juvenile delinquents, Castro, television commercials and the modern novel, people tend to take the gloomy view and they welcome someone who comes along and makes them even sorrier for themselves than they would have been without assistance.

And in the last of this trio, an article for **Cavalier** for April 1965 entitled **A Cool Look at Snails**, he was in much more of a teasing mood:

It is always a red-letter day for me when the income-tax demand comes in, for I love to give the Government of my plenty, bless its dear old heart. What's mine is yours is my motto. But, though heaven knows I don't begrudge these panhandlers their annual hundred thousand or couple of hundred thousand or whatever it is, I do find myself agreeing with Senator Byrd of Virginia that they should be more careful what they spend the money on.

I am quite agreeable to them wanting to study "the diving reflex and volume receptors in the seal" at my expense because I admired Elizabeth Seal in *Irma la Douce* so much and naturally would like to hear all about her volume receptors, but quite a bit of what I made last year by the sweat of my brow will, according to the Senator, go toward finding "ways of using sunfish to control snails", a project which has little appeal for me.

So now we know.

Occasionally, Wodehouse had second thoughts about the wisdom of including a sly dig. Or, he may merely have decided that the gem he had devised was so good that he wanted to keep it back to enhance another volume at a later date. One example can be found in the history of **Galahad at Blandings**[19], published without any references to taxes or tax collectors whatsoever.

BUT, in the typed manuscript in the British Library Manuscripts Collection, there was a reference in the draft which was scrubbed out. It appears on page 99, and goes as follows:

His sympathy was kindled. He himself was a man who felt depressed himself for weeks after he had paid his annual income tax.

AND, in the hand-written notes also in the British Library, there are two examples of thinking relating to tax as a way of introducing a potential character in the text. In fact, the character for whom the excuse was suggested did not appear in the final scenario or book:

draft notes, page 1; 27/5/63

> *Try this, Bunting the lawyer is at Bl to do Ld E's income tax. Souse is his nephew and B has some financial hold on him and has told him not to drink, or suppose hero is a young barrister hoping to be briefed by Bunting in big case. Then hero cd knock off drink in order to ingratiate himself. He has told B he is a teetotaller.*

draft notes, page 3; 29/5/63

> *The blow-out. Hero has been posing as someone else. Bunting turns up to do Ld E's income tax & tells hero (in front of Lady X) that he has been trying to get in touch with him to brief him in some case.*

We will never know whether it was the influence that Wodehouse had on Bolton by letter and conversation that made Bolton include the following two Wodehousean passages in his very readable novel, **Gracious Living Limited**[20]:

> "I know you think I'm a silly old woman with a silly old car, not to mention a silly Poodle Parlour, but I'm determined to keep the old flag flying as long as I can."

> "In the meanwhile you are barely making enough to pay your taxes."

> It was painfully true and Aunt Jo knew it. Taxes had mounted steadily as the years went on and the cost of living also went up ...

And later,

> "And do all these services combine into a nice fat income?"

> "They add up, but unfortunately, working against them, are mortgage payments, taxes, and the ever-rising rates."

In the story *Life With Freddie*[21], Wodehouse returns to a well-used theme, ie an attempt to smuggle a diamond necklace through customs in a Mickey Mouse with a head that unscrews, in order to evade import duties. It is probably fair to say that the most obvious instances in any of Wodehouse's writings of attempts to evade taxes rather than to grumble about them, or save them through wishful thinking, relate to import and excise duties, which can be saved by successful smuggling, (with the apparent approval of almost the whole world).

The topic is referred to intermittently throughout the story, and extracts would not do the subject justice.

The search for a tax-free source of income has a fascination which is occasionally explored, but when an idea was put forward in **Company For Henry**[22] it was not strictly in accordance with legal principles!

> *Algy Martyn is speaking to Bill Hardy.*
>
> "...We advertise in all the local papers that we are willing for a small fee to give advice in the matters of the heart..... At half a crown a go we should be pulling the stuff in, and no income tax to pay, for all transactions would be carried through in untraceable postal orders...."

Occasionally Wodehouse suggested that paying tax was a little like going to a public school, see for example his essay *Thoughts on the Income Tax* in **Louder and Funnier,** when he suggested that it should be possible to get one's super-tax colours. In **A Pelican at Blandings**[23], he slightly changed the concept, putting forward the view that a son would seek to follow his father's footsteps if he were a high-rate taxpayer:

> Had he [Trout] been the son of someone humble in the lower tax brackets, he would have gone through the years as a blameless and contented filing clerk.

The plot of **The Girl in Blue**[24] involved an attempt, yet again, by an elder son to maintain his stately pile, but this time his young brother has made a success in a professional position:

> The Scropes of Mellingham Hall had functioned more than comfortably through a number of centuries, but the present owner of that ancient pile, as he often said, did not know which way to turn, all he had to console him was the memory of the costly fun he had enjoyed in his youth. Willoughby, the younger son, who after the fashion of younger sons had been thrust out into the world to earn his living, was now in the highest income tax bracket: Crispin, the heir, was forced to take in paying guests in order to make both ends meet: and now there was yawning between those ends a gap of two hundred and three pounds six shillings and fourpence.

Willoughby was thus worried about taxes, and rather like Wodehouse himself assumed everyone else was, as in this conversation with Crispin:

> "But let's talk of something else," he said, "beginning with what brings you up here like this, when it's unheard of for you to come up to London. Is it business?" "
>
> "No, not exactly business, Bill."
>
> "Income tax?"
>
> "No, not income tax."

The Wodehouse Code, that a man should not sponge, or be thought capable of sponging, on a woman, was tested twice in this book. First, by Jane Hunnicutt, whose unexpected inheritance seemed to undo the matrimonial aspirations of the almost penniless Jerry West, until they were rescued by the US marines in the totally unexpected guise of the IRS:

Jerry was frankly appalled. To Jane Hunnicut, he presumed, these pennies from heaven, if that was where old Mr Donahue had gone, had brought happiness and rejoicing, for even in this era of depressed currencies between one and two million dollars is always well worth having, but he saw in her sudden access to the higher income tax brackets the crashing of all his hopes and dreams.

It was Willoughby who explained the route by which all was not to be lost:

Jane Hunnicutt gets everything, but the United States Federal sharks will see to it that that isn't much. The late Mr Donahue appears to have been one of those men who don't approve of the income tax. He hadn't paid his for fifteen years. You can imagine what the sharks will do with a case like that. They'll have a field day. Add debts, liabilities for surtax, capital gains tax, death duties and all the rest of it, and there won't be a lot left. The same thing happened to a client of mine the other day. His gross estate was four hundred thousand pounds, and they whittled it down to something like seven thousand net. If Jane Hunnicut gets away with about that, she'll be lucky.

The final reference in this book was more general, Barney speaking to Crispin:

"Crips! What's the matter? What is it? What's wrong? ... Tell me," she said.

"I'm in an awful fix," said Crispin.

Her mind leapt to the obvious explanation.

"Money?"

"Yes"

"A bill?"

"Yes"

"How much?"

"A hundred pounds."

"Is that all?" said Barney, relieved. In the income tax bracket to which she belonged a hundred pounds or its equivalent in dollars was something which fell into the category of small change.

And when Crispin and Barney agreed to marry, it didn't seem like a breach of the code that she was wealthy and he wasn't!

It was not often that Bertie Wooster was given *carte blanche* to think for himself and carry out the consequences of that thought process. In **Much Obliged, Jeeves**[25], he prepared a strategy to woo voters on behalf of Ginger Winship, and when confronted by his first canvassee started to put it into practice:

> Over an after-dinner smoke on the previous night Ginger had filled me in on what his crowd proposed to do when they got down to it. They were going, he said, to cut taxes to the bone, straighten out our foreign policy, double our export trade, have two cars in the garage and two chickens in the pot for everyone and give the pound the shot in the arm it had been clamouring for for years. Than which, we both agreed, nothing could be sweeter, and I saw no reason to suppose that the McCorkadale gargoyle would not feel the same. I began, therefore, by asking her if she had a vote, and she said Yes, of course, and I said Well that was fine, because if she hadn't, the point of my arguments would have been largely lost.

"An excellent thing, I've always thought, giving women the vote," I proceeded heartily, and she said — rather nastily, it seemed to me — that she was glad I approved. "When you cast yours, if cast is the word I want, I strongly advise you to cast it in favour of Ginger Winship."

"On what do you base that advice?"

She couldn't have given me a better cue. She had handed it to me on a plate with watercress round it. Like a flash I went into my sales talk, mentioning Ginger's attitude towards taxes, our foreign policy, our export trade, cars in the garage, chickens in the pot and first aid for the poor old pound, and was shocked to observe an entire absence of enthusiasm on her part. Not a ripple appeared on the stern and rockbound coast of her map. She looked like Aunt Agatha listening to the boy Wooster trying to explain away a drawing-room window broken by a cricket ball.

I pressed her closely, or do I mean keenly.

"You want taxes cut, don't you?"

"I do."

The twin themes of tax deductions and professional advice crop up again during a conversation between Aunt Dahlia, Bertie and Jeeves about L P Runkle's porringer, and how much "blackmail" money he may be prepared to pay to recover it. Jeeves expresses an opinion:

"... He will scarcely disburse a hundred or even fifty thousand in order to recover it."

"Of course he won't," I said, as enchanted with his lucidity, as he had been with mine. It was the sort of thing you have to pay topnotchers at the Bar a king's

234

ransom for. "He'll simply say "Easy come, easy go" and write it off as a business loss, possibly consulting his legal adviser as to whether he can deduct it from his income tax. Thank you, Jeeves. You've straightened everything out in your customary masterly manner ... "

The repetition of the plot of **The Luck of the Bodkins**, referred to in connection with the short story *Life With Freddie*, recurs in **Pearls, Girls and Monty Bodkin**[26], but principally to establish the characters and their relationship with each other. There are numerous references to the need to evade customs duties to ensure peace in the various households, but nothing new which warrants quotation. Except when Dolly Molloy is promoting her idea of transferring ownership of a rope of pearls to a partnership of herself and her husband Soapy:

"Remember that rope of pearls of Mrs Llewellyn's? You saw it often enough at the Casino. It must be worth fifty thousand dollars at least. Fifty thousand smackers, honey, and no income tax to pay on it."

There were also vague hints at reminiscence of his *All About The Income Tax* essay in a comment made by Ephraim Trout to Joe Pickering about the dangers of marriage, in **Bachelors Anonymous**[24]:

"Like so many young men ... you have allowed yourself to become ensnared by a pretty face, never asking yourself if the person you are hoping to marry is capable of making out your income tax return and can be relied on to shovel snow while you are curled up beside the fire with a novel of suspense."

His final publication during his lifetime was **Aunts Aren't Gentlemen**[27], and it seems fitting that the two references he makes to tax in that book involve first, a purported professional adviser (Jeeves, impersonating a non-existent solicitor):

235

"Mr Wooster has ample means. It seems scarcely likely, therefore, that he would have attempted to obtain a mere five pounds from you. I can speak with authority as to Mr Wooster's financial standing, for I am his solicitor and prepare his annual income tax return."

and later, the unchanged views of Uncle Tom Travers on income tax, as expressed in a letter to Bertie:

Then came three pages about the weather, the income tax (which he dislikes) and the recent purchases he had made for his collection of old silver...

I don't see how there could be a more fitting ending to the review of Wodehouse's published views on the subject of taxes, as Uncle Tom's views undoubtedly reflected his own, as well, perhaps, as the views of 90% of his readership.

Footnotes

1   Till the Clouds Roll By 1946, MGM
2   1951, Herbert Jenkins
3   1952, Herbert Jenkins
4   1991, Michael Joseph
5   1952, Herbert Jenkins
6   1953, Herbert Jenkins
7   1954, Herbert Jenkins
8   May, 20, 1953
9   1956, Simon & Schuster
10 1957, Herbert Jenkins
11 1932, Faber and Faber
12 1957, Herbert Jenkins
13 1957, Herbert Jenkins
14 1957, in **A Few Quick Ones** 1959, Herbert Jenkins
15 1960, Herbert Jenkins
16 1961, Herbert Jenkins
17 1963, Herbert Jenkins
18 1964, Herbert Jenkins

APPENDIX — THE TECHNICAL BACKGROUND

In this Appendix, an attempt will be made to outline the various tax traps which Wodehouse faced during the inter-war period, the time during which his contretemps with the Revenue authorities were the greatest.

It is not suggested that the following represents a full technical analysis of the various matters discussed since that could produce a book on its own, and would in any event be of little interest to most Wodehouse readers. But an awareness of the complexity of some of the problems faced can help readers to understand why he may have adopted certain courses of action to seek to reduce tax liabilities, and to appreciate that, on the whole, they might easily have done something very similar if they had received the same advice in the same circumstances.

TAX STATUS — UK and US

In both the UK and US, an individual's exposure to personal taxation depends on his tax status in any tax year, which is the calendar year in the US and the period from April 6 one year to April 5 in the next in the UK. This would be determined in each country on the basis of two separate factors. In the UK, these factors are "domicile" and "residence" (although a further concept of *ordinary residence* can complicate the matter and be of some importance in some years). In the US the factors are "Citizenship" and "residence" but this latter term carries a different definition from that used in the UK.

The UK position

Under British law, in the period up to and beyond the second world war, a person took the domicile of his or her father in the absence of any other rule and despite Wodehouse's father's career in Hong Kong, it seems certain that he would have retained UK domicile for tax and other purposes.

239

It is actually — or was until a recent change in the law — incredibly difficult to lose a domicile of origin. Simply put, one has to sever all connections with the country of origin *and*, of equal importance, to be able to demonstrate and prove an intention to take up permanent domicile elsewhere.

Wodehouse's movements in the inter-war period were such that he could not have lost his UK domicile of origin, although it is probable that this would have been achieved when he took US citizenship in 1955. Ethel would have taken her husband's domicile on marriage — the recent changes in the law which modified this rule in some circumstances would not have affected her in any event — and thus would also have been treated as domiciled in the UK as long as he was, even if her intentions for the future had been different.

A UK domiciled person is taxed on his or her worldwide income, with many modifications to this basic principle, particularly in tax years in which he or she was not resident in the UK. The residence position of each spouse is determined separately, depending on their movements and certain other factors. It is therefore just possible that Ethel might have been resident in the UK in years when PG alone was in the US for substantial spells.

One major benefit for PG was that he could avoid paying UK tax on earnings abroad if they were not remitted to the UK during a period of residence. An understanding of the meaning of "residence" was thus important to Wodehouse. He knew he would be resident if he spent 183 days in the UK in any tax year. He also knew that he would be treated as resident if he averaged three months a year in the UK for four years, or if he maintained a house available for his use and paid any visits at all — whether or not he stayed in the house!

One of the defences apparently put forward on his behalf in the UK tax litigation was that the house in Norfolk Street which had been bought in his name had been acquired, not for his own occupation, but for that of his step-daughter, Leonora. It may therefore not in any case have been available for his use, but that argument was strengthened by the fact that she had rented it out for successive three-year periods. He seems generally to have tried quite hard to keep within the rules — hence his plaintive letters to Leonora and others:

26 April 1934 to Olive Grills

I have to be out of England for a year owing to some income tax technicality ...

19 December 1934 to Leonora

I shall be glad when April comes and I can get over to England ...

6 March 1935 to Bill Townend

I shall come to England as soon after April 5 as I can manage.

Despite Barry Phelps' view, as expressed in **P G Wodehouse — Man and Myth**[1] that "numerous letters show that he slipped over to England from Le Touquet on the Channel ferry to spend the weekend at Shipbourne on numerous occasions in the thirties, apparently without telling the taxman", it would seem that at least in 1934/35 he was quite careful. An analysis of PG's known movements does not really support Barry's conclusion that the visits were generally surreptitious — the need to keep away from the country for the entire year would only arise if a house was available for him. For example, if Ethel was still in the UK, or if they had taken a lease of a house for a period, and the lease was not yet up.

The US position

Until he obtained citizenship, PG was an alien for US tax purposes, but would still have been subject to tax in respect of each year for which he received taxable income either as a "resident alien" or as a "non-resident alien". At that time, a non-resident alien was an

241

alien who had not become resident, ie a "transient" or "sojourner". Whether a person was a transient was determined by intentions with regard to the length and nature of a person's stay. A mere floating intention, indefinite as to time, to return to another country, particularly coupled with a home in the US, would not enable a person to remain a transient. If a person came to the US for a definite purpose, of such a nature that an extended stay may be necessary for its accomplishment, he would become a resident even though it may be his intention to return to his domicile abroad when the purpose has been completed. Finally, in the absence of exceptional circumstances, an alien whose stay is limited in time by the immigration laws, will be treated as a transient.

Wodehouse may well have been regarded as resident in the US in those years in which he lived in Hollywood, having taken a house, such as 1930, 1931 and 1937, and in such years he would have been exposed to US tax on his worldwide income, with only limited exceptions. In other years he may well have sought to make absolutely sure he was non-resident, as this significantly reduced both the scope of the US tax charge (effectively restricting it to tax on US source income) and until 1937, when the rules were changed, kept the tax rate down to a maximum of 10% of gross income. This was collected by means of a withholding tax which was treated as a final liability, in contrast to the position for a resident who would have been taxed at full US individual tax rates.

As in the UK, Ethel's US residence status would have been determined each year, independently of PG's, and she would have been responsible for filing tax returns appropriate to her status and sources and level of income.

The Relevance of France

Since nothing is simple in tax, it would be wrong to assume that, with the US and the UK both determining residence independently, the Wodehouses would each have been resident in one of the countries each year but not both. It would be quite possible for them to be treated as resident in both or neither during the same period, a result facilitated by the difference, previously explained, in the dates of the tax years in the UK and the US.

To reduce the likelihood of being treated as resident in one — or more particularly both — countries, PG hit on the idea of basing himself in France. The great thing, from his point of view, was that France had a territorial basis of taxation, which means that they only taxed French source income, not worldwide income. And although many of his books (at least 10 between 1929 and 1938) were translated into French, and sold there, total sales and thus royalties were, like the Canadian sales of Aileen Peavey, not large.

If such an advantageous tax system could be coupled with the country's proximity to the UK, one had what was evidently a very interesting compromise. If he could remain non-resident for both UK and US purposes, he would reduce his taxable income to that derived from the UK, the US and France, *and* benefit from low rates of tax in the US, at least until 1937.

And should readers not be thankful for the circumstances which gave us those brilliant, masterly, first few sentences in **The Luck of the Bodkins**[2]:

> Into the face of the young man who sat on the terrace of the Hotel Magnifique at Cannes there had crept a look of furtive shame, the shifty, hangdog look which announces that an Englishman is about to talk French ... Although he knew that it was going to make his nose tickle, he said:
>
> "Er, garçon."

THE USE OF COMPANIES

One of the ways in which Wodehouse sought to reduce his UK tax exposure was to form a US company, **Jeeves Dramatics, Inc**, in 1927. This was intended to receive book royalties. Even if he were found to be resident in the UK in any year, he hoped to show that he personally was not entitled to these funds, and could not be taxed on them.

Another approach which he tried was to establish a company in Switzerland (referred to as "SwissCo"), and sell to it (for a period of four years from 25 April, 1934) all earnings, copyrights, royalties, commissions and other revenues on the sale of literary, theatrical or cinematographic productions, thereby hoping that personal taxes arising on him in the US or the UK would be reduced and replaced by smaller withholding taxes on payments to SwissCo.

Although the US Revenue were fully aware of the existence of SwissCo from the outset, they still felt the need — in the 1940's — to raise tax assessments outrageously accusing Wodehouse of fraudulent actions in relation to his dealings with SwissCo (see chapter 7).

One practical problem with using "personal" companies for reasons such as tax mitigation is that the ground rules have to be set in clear language, and the procedures followed by all involved. It is evident from the correspondence at the time that the company administration, particularly in the hands of John W Rumsey, was somewhat amateurish, and payments, etc, were made which were not wholly in accordance with those expected by the professional advisers.

There is certainly nothing wrong with using companies in this way, but their existence creates risks, and sometimes the problems represented by those risks materialise.

HUSBAND AND WIFE

In the US, citizens have an option of filing joint tax returns as a family of husband and wife or as separate persons. Depending on the level of income of the two partners, the joint return might give a lower overall tax bill, especially if the income of one spouse was not sufficient to utilise that spouse's tax deductions, personal tax allowances and lower rate tax bands. But no similar option was available to aliens, even resident aliens taxable on their worldwide income.

So for periods when the Wodehouses were resident, or expecting to be resident, in the US, PG wished to achieve a similar benefit, in order to be in no worse position than his American colleagues. His advisers discussed two courses of action with him:

1 First, they explored whether, as while working with MGM he was resident in California, a community property state, he could successfully argue that his wife was automatically entitled to half his income by process of local law. After extensive investigation by his advisers, they concluded that it would not be safe to rely on this idea, as the applicable law for this purpose was that relating to where he was domiciled — at the time, England, which was not a community property country.

2 Secondly, they considered the suggestion that he enter into agreements to give Ethel all, or a proportion of, his rights to certain royalties from specified productions. They believed that, provided the gifts were completed before any income-generating contracts had been signed in relation to the stories, when the income was paid to her, it should validly be treated as her income for tax purposes. This idea was pursued, and was one of the matters considered in the Appeals described in the text.

CAPITAL GAINS OR TAXABLE INCOME

One of the post-war phenomena has been the imposition of tax on capital gains, which was not generally the case between the wars. In England, for example, there was a limited attack in 1962, and a full capital gains regime was enacted in 1965. In the US, capital gains have generally been taxable on residents, but at favourable rates, and often not taxable on non-residents because of the known practical difficulties of collecting the tax. Of course, human nature being what it is, the result of something being taxable and something very similar either being not taxable at all, or at lower rates, is going to be a series of highly technical arguments about which side of the dividing line certain transactions fall, arguments which are very lucrative for the acting professional advisers where significant tax is at stake.

The main point in the Wodehouse tax saga related to sales of his serials to magazines such as *Saturday Evening Post*, *Colliers*, and *Cosmopolitan*, for which he received lump sum payments while retaining book rights, overseas (other than Canadian) rights, theatrical rights, etc.

As Wodehouse himself put it during the negotiations with the IRS, and whilst the cases were being litigated,

> *The point at issue is does the money I got for Saturday Evening Post serials count as income? Any normal person would say yes of course it does but the Government is solemnly deliberating the point and its quite possible they will refund me all the money I have paid in taxes on those serials.*[3]

and after the decision had been announced by the Supreme Court that the IRS were right,

> *I couldn't believe in my most optimistic moments that any Government would let me get away with the argument that Saturday Evening Post serials weren't income but were outright sales.*[4]

SOURCE OF INCOME

For US tax purposes, a non-resident alien was only chargeable to tax on income which was considered to have a US source. Sales of serial rights to *Saturday Evening Post*, *Cosmopolitan*, etc, covered Canada as well as the US and the question arose as to whether, if the sale proceeds were income (as they proved to be), part of the proceeds could be attributed to the Canadian rights and thus be outside the US tax net.

One of the difficulties with a problem like this is how, if the point is conceded in principle, the value of the Canadian rights can be calculated in the absence of a separate figure for the Canadian consideration appearing in the contract.

THE POWERS OF THE REVENUE AUTHORITIES

The Revenue authorities exist to administer the tax system, to collect the government's staff of life, and increasingly to both counteract the ingenuity of the professional tax advisers, (which grew steadily between the wars and since), and monitor the activities of those taxpayers not bound by the ethical code or moral suasion of a professional body. Universally perceived as the taker-away, and never the giver, they go about disguised as the Inland Revenue in the UK, and the Internal Revenue Service in the US. But however efficiently, politely and carefully they do their job, they are seen in our minds as a blackshorted band of pickpockets, probably under the executive direction of Lord Sidcup.

When one is thinking about the Revenue authorities scrutinizing the activities of taxpayers, does one see their approach as "Live and Let Live?" No, one doesn't. Even though from time to time we may sympathise with their problems, we put their attitude down to that of school prefects like Gethryn, in **A Prefect's Uncle**[5], in his dealings with fellow students such as Monk and Danvers.

A brief extract from Chapter 12 should help to make the point:

> *In the first place, [Gethryn] reasoned within himself, if Monk and Danvers were doing anything, it was probably wrong, and ought to be stopped. Gethryn*

*always had the feeling that it was his duty to go and
see what Monk and Danvers were doing, and tell them
they mustn't.*

Since these words were written in 1903, at a time when
Wodehouse had not yet visited the US, he could not have gained
his inspiration for the concept from his experiences of the IRS.
But there can be little doubt that he came to view that body in the
same light!

One must remain objective, however, and concede that Revenue
Departments do have a very difficult but valid assignment.
Virtually all taxpayers, whether they admit it or not, share Tom
Travers's reluctance to shell out for their tax dues, and when they
hide their liabilities unlawfully, the Revenue will have right on their
side where their own interpretation of the law is ultimately found
to be correct.

But in their role as tax-gatherers they are too often unsympathetic
to the reasonable view of many taxpayers that when the law says
"X'" it means "X'"even if the IRS thinks it can be read as meaning
"Y". Or sometimes the IRS may go further, and claim merely that
it was meant to mean "Y", even if it clearly says "X". In these
cases, the IRS approach reflects that of Erb in **Uncle Fred in the
Springtime**[6], the "great beefy brute" dangled before Pongo
Twistleton who "acted in an executive capacity on behalf of
George Budd", a bookie who was Pongo's creditor at the time.

The Revenue's ability to compromise a settlement, and the
resources behind them (to the taxpayer seemingly unrestricted),
which can be used to pursue a case through the Courts, combine
to tempt certain Revenue staff to be over-bearing, threatening to
cause the taxpayer to incur heavy professional fees to defend its
integrity if it does not accede to a demand for more tax.

Because the Press is not able to report tax cases which go
smoothly and are settled amicably or with minimal enquiry (and
wouldn't bother even if it could), the cases about which the public
becomes aware are the relatively few where the Revenue officers

have overstepped the bounds of reasonable behaviour, and the good, fair and responsible approach of the majority of Officers should be borne in mind. In the UK, certainly, the experience of most qualified tax advisers is that it is only a small minority of Revenue officials who are unreasonable.

But the attitude of the majority does, unfortunately, pall against the worst mistakes made by those who succumb to the overpowering temptation to abuse power. It is partly a resources problem; the perceived immense resources of the public services mean that not only do they have to act reasonably, they have to be seen to act reasonably, and they must not impose unfair standards of proof or administration on the taxpayer. All taxpayers should be treated as innocent until proved guilty, but when the Revenue authorities add two and two and make any number higher than four, the taxpayer may be left having to prove a negative in order to avoid paying excessive tax charges. This was the situation in which Wodehouse found himself in relation to the question of whether tax returns had been filed for the years 1923 and 1924.

THE SHAM TRANSACTION

The need to prove a negative is all too common when taxpayers are faced with allegations concerning one ingenious concept which was developed by the IRS and the US Tax Courts many years ago. Because of some very enlightened judgements in the past — to the effect that no taxpayer is required to so arrange his affairs that the Inland Revenue can put the greatest possible shovel in his assets — this idea only started to be given any serious credence in the UK in the late 1970's and 1980's, and even then, its impact was reduced by later House of Lords [the UK Supreme Appeal Court] decisions in the taxpayer's favour.

The concept is that of the "sham" transaction. In extreme cases, it means that a perfectly valid, properly executed transaction — in full legal form, with full legal effect and in accordance with the intentions of the parties involved — can be ignored if the tax authorities feel that it has no commercial substance, and really achieves nothing but a beneficial tax treatment for one or both parties to it. As can be seen in the main text (chapters 6 & 7), two of the aspects of the Wodehouse US Tax Cases concerned alleged sham transactions, and this in turn led to unjustified accusations of tax fraud.

THE TAX COURTS

In England and Wales, when a taxpayer does not like the enthusiasm shown by the Revenue in "trying to sneak your little all", he or she can appeal to a series of Courts, at an ever-increasing cost, which is substantially for the account of the ultimate loser. There is a choice of court at the first level, but after this first hearing — which is before either the General or Special Commissioners (for personal taxes) or the VAT Tribunal (for sales taxes) — the route for any appeal is the Chancery Division, the Court of Appeal and the House of Lords. It is important to appreciate that only the Commissioners can hear and decide questions of fact — the higher courts' jurisdiction is limited to determining whether the application of the law to those facts is correct.

In Scotland the procedure is abbreviated, the Chancery and Court of Appeal steps being replaced by a single hearing before the Court of Session, while the procedure in Northern Ireland is similar to that in Scotland. In England and Wales, it is possible for the taxpayer (or the Revenue) to win on a unanimous verdict at the Commissioners' hearing, the Chancery Court and the Court of Appeal, only to lose 3-2 in the decider in the House of Lords. (Since there is just one judge at Chancery level, but three at the Court of Appeal, the "loser" may actually win the support of six judges out of nine.)

So the UK system has its anomalies and weaknesses, but at least it does not have the same degree of similarity to *Alice in Wonderland* as that demonstrated in Wodehouse's case by the US Courts.

His Appeal started in the Tax Court, and appeals on points of law were lodged from there to the Court of Appeal. Because he had filed tax returns for different years in different locations, his appeals went to different Circuits of the Court of Appeal. The Fourth Circuit found for Wodehouse on one issue and for the IRS on another. How many readers were astute enough to have guessed that the Second Circuit found for the IRS on the first issue and for Wodehouse on the second?

No wonder the poor man was confused.

Footnotes

1 1992, Macdonald
2 1935, Herbert Jenkins
3 Letter to W Townend, January 15, 1949
4 Letter to W Townend
5 1903, A & C Black
6 1939, Herbert Jenkins

INDEX